Instant
MOTIVATION

Instant
MOTIVATION

BRIAN CLEGG

**KOGAN
PAGE**

To Nic and Sarah Cope – musical motivators par excellence

First published in 2000

Apart from any fair dealing for the purposes of research or private study, or criticism or review, as permitted under the Copyright, Designs and Patents Act 1988, this publication may only be reproduced, stored or transmitted, in any form or by any means, with the prior permission in writing of the publishers, or in the case of reprographic reproduction in accordance with the terms and licences issued by the CLA. Enquiries concerning reproduction outside these terms should be sent to the publishers at the undermentioned addresses:

Kogan Page Limited
120 Pentonville Road
London
N1 9JN
UK

Stylus Publishing Inc.
22883 Quicksilver Drive
Sterling
VA 20166–2012
USA

© Brian Clegg, 2000

The right of Brian Clegg to be identified as the author of this work has been asserted by him in accordance with the Copyright, Designs and Patents Act 1988.

British Library Cataloguing in Publication Data

A CIP record for this book is available from the British Library.

ISBN 0 7494 3101 6

Typeset by Jo Brereton, Primary Focus, Haslington, Cheshire
Printed and bound by Clays Ltd, St Ives plc

Contents

4 Large scale 25

5 The exercises 33

1

MOTIVATION

EMPOWERING OR BRAINWASHING?

It can be so depressing – you know that your staff, your peers, your boss, your friends and family can achieve more, and yet they don't. Often all that is lacking is the motivation to succeed. This book contains a toolkit of tried and tested techniques to increase motivation. Because motivation has to be applied on the spot, whenever needed, it is a natural subject for the *Instant* formula of providing a package of quick-to-read and quick-to-implement ideas that can be started right away. *Instant Motivation* contains over 70 exercises, each short enough to fit into a few spare minutes at any time of the day. As part of the *Instant* series (including *Instant Teamwork*, *Instant Creativity* and *Instant Time Management*), it is a handy resource for individuals, team leaders, managers and trainers.

Motivation is one of those terms that can mean very different things depending on exactly where you sit. According to the dictionary it's about giving someone a motive or an incentive or, rather more darkly, about inducing something. If I am motivating someone else, it's easy to see that it is positive. When was there ever anything wrong with an incentive? If I am on the receiving end of motivation, there is a danger of feeling manipulated – not so much given an incentive as forced into a particular behavioural pattern by sleight of hand. And because we are dealing with human behaviour, this is a particularly sensitive issue.

Part of the skill of motivation is ensuring that there is a win–win outcome. You should feel that you are achieving your goals by motivating others. If you have staff, for example, you might hope to get better quality work out of them by motivating them. Those who are being motivated should either not notice it at all (and thus be pleased with their own success), or consider it a positive support, increasing their job satisfaction. Because of the fine line between support and manipulation, motivation isn't a skill that can be codified as a set of rules. Instead, like many of the *Instant* books' subjects, it is based on guiding principles and practical experience at putting those principles into action.

WHO CAN WE MOTIVATE?

The target of your effort could be anyone – anyone can be motivated – and you can be the one to do it. In fact, the potential for motivation starts with yourself. Self-motivation is very important, but although there are some overlaps with motivating others, it is probably best treated separately alongside other self-development skills like assertiveness.

If we confine ourselves to looking outwards, motivation is an extremely powerful tool reaching far beyond the traditional image of motivating your staff at work. You can motivate your family when a holiday is flagging. You can motivate an individual to greater efforts, or a team to pull together. You can motivate a whole company to buy into the board's dreams and aspirations – or you can motivate a huge, diverse group like 'your customers' to buy more of your product. Advertising and marketing fall outside the scope of this book, but there is a strong overlap between some of the mechanisms of motivation and best practice in these disciplines.

WHAT'S THE POINT?

The cynical view of motivation is that it is a matter of subtle manipulation; that motivation is just a way of getting other people to do what you want them to do, ideally without them realizing that this is your aim. This is the view of motivation of a manager I once knew, who thought that staff were more productive if they thought you cared about them, and so maintained that it was very important to fool them into thinking you cared. Insincere, faked motivation will deliver to a point, for a while, but then it will founder.

To have a deep, lasting effect motivation has to be something more – something of benefit to all involved. Yes, those involved in doing the motivation want to get something out of it, but not just more efficiency or better quality output – and certainly not a set of robots who respond automatically to the party line. They want those who are being motivated to get real satisfaction out of what they are doing. Like it or not, truly effective motivation can't just give lip-service to the feelings and desires of those being motivated, it has to have real concern for the recipients as people.

This can make motivation sound painfully woolly and touchy-feely. If you are reading this book, you are looking for a practical business tool, not a social worker's charter. Don't worry – practical business applications are what it's all about, but it is always necessary to bear in mind that motivation is about people, not numbers or data or machinery. The human element will always be present. Hopefully, for most people involved in leading or managing staff this won't be a problem – isn't it part of why you wanted to be a manager in the first place? Part, in fact, of your own motivation.

WHO IS *INSTANT MOTIVATION* FOR?

Being primarily a business book, *Instant Motivation* is aimed at anyone who has to work with anyone else. They don't have to be people you manage, or even people who work for the same company. The targets of your motivation could be your boss, or the queue at your check-in desk – or anyone else who comes into the sphere of your work activity. As we have seen, good motivation is an important tool, not to impose your will, but to bring out the best in people. Unless you work alone on a subsistence-level croft on a remote island, *Instant Motivation* is for you.

USING THIS BOOK

The techniques and introductory chapters look at motivation on three different levels, each with different requirements. The first level of motivation concerns the individual, giving someone the encouragement to make that extra mile. The second focuses on the team, pulling together a group with a common aim to achieve success. The third is large-scale motivation – working with a whole set of people at a conference or other large gathering. Such a group hasn't the same focus as a team, but needs more general motivation. The techniques in the book are inspirational and fun without adopting the over-the-top style that makes some motivational material of the 1970s and 1980s seem artificial to a modern audience.

Each exercise in *Instant Motivation* is presented in a standard format, with brief details of any preparation required, running time, resources used and the timescale of its application, followed by a description of the exercise itself. Next come suggestions for feedback, comments on the outcome and possible variations on the technique. The final part of the entry is the star rating. This is a quick reference to show how the particular exercise impacts on motivation of individuals, teams and large groups – and how much fun it is likely to be. As much as possible, to keep with the 'instant' theme, the exercises require minimal preparation, but some exercises requiring a little more work beforehand are included as they can sometimes be particularly effective. Note that timings are a minimum – you can take longer over most of the exercises if it is appropriate.

How you use the exercises very much depends on your approach to life. There is nothing wrong with working through the whole book in sequence. Alternatively, the tables in the Appendix offer a number of ways of picking an exercise. There is a random selection table as a way of dipping into the exercises without getting into a rut. And there are tables arranging the exercises by how well they scored in the various star ratings. Use the exercises however they best fit with your schedule with the proviso that becoming effective at motivation requires regular practice, and that you shouldn't skip an exercise because it hasn't an immediate application – you might not have the chance to read a book next time you need to employ some motivation. With motivation, spontaneity is extremely important – it's a classic *Instant* topic.

2

ONE TO ONE

THE INDIVIDUAL

One of the hardest motivational challenges is dealing with an individual. You may be coaching an under-performer or helping someone with low self-esteem. You may be dealing with a very talented individual who is under-using those talents. Whatever the need for motivation, the starting point has to be that you are dealing with an individual. I've intentionally used that word a lot in this paragraph. That's because in most companies, there's a lot of historical baggage to overcome. Let's spend a moment looking at it.

Those who have seen re-runs of the 1960s' cult TV show *The Prisoner* will recall the recurrent cry of Patrick McGoohan's central character Number Six – 'I am not a number'. This reduction of the individual to a faceless component was not just a feature of fantasy TV-settings, but the devastatingly costly outcome of one of the biggest mistakes humanity has ever made. (If this all sounds too philosophical for you, skip the next couple of paragraphs, but remember we are dealing with people and people issues are at the core of motivation.)

Until very recent times, those in charge have been happy to regard the rest of humanity as a set of interchangeable pawns. The general attitude to war, to slavery, to much of the class system prevalent until very recently (and still common in some parts of the world) makes this very obvious. Despite the entirely contrary ethics that form the basis of Western society, the ruling classes have managed to ignore the individuality of the rest.

When mechanization transformed business, there was no reason to challenge this picture. In fact, the new world of production lines and mass manufacturing seemed to require the picture of the worker as just another cog in the great machine. Films from the period when mechanization was sweeping business, like Fritz Lang's still powerful *Metropolis*, portray the workers quite literally as parts of the machine. Of course, no one thinks like that any more, do they? Yet the legacy of that past is still with us.

Consciously or unconsciously, most companies still do a lot to make sure that their employees realize that they are cogs in the machine. They issue them with staff numbers, job descriptions, organization charts and scores that show the relative value of their jobs. When looking at pay rises they give ratings, perhaps normalized to make sure there's a fair distribution, and make sure that different managers aren't dealing with their staff differently – as if, perhaps, they were individuals.

But that's an unfair picture, isn't it? All these things are done for very sensible reasons. Because the computer needs a number, or the system will only work if we have a uniform system of ratings. Yet most of these sensible reasons are derived from a senseless value structure that comes back to thinking of people as interchangeable components. All too often still, senior managers think of an organization, then fit people into it (we've got x analysts, y admin staff and z managers) rather than building the organization around the people. Why? Not because it delivers the best results; it doesn't. It's because of that historical baggage and because it's easier to do.

Now, though, we live in a world where what is easiest isn't always good enough. We need to get the best out of people, which means treating them as individuals not as components. It's trite, but it's true – everyone really is different, and so getting the best out of them means treating everyone differently. If that presents a problem for the systems, tough. If you want to survive you are going to have to change the systems. Ideally, you also want to do it because you want people actually to enjoy their work – but even if you don't, the pragmatic truth is that you need to deal with each person differently. They *are* individuals.

ONE SIZE FITS ALL

Taking the message of the previous section, we've immediately got a problem when looking at motivating an individual. If everyone is different, and we can't treat them as interchangeable components any more, how is it possible to make any progress? Doesn't this mean you need a book called *Instant Motivation of Jean Rutter* this morning, and another completely different book called *Instant Motivation of Dennis Taylor* this afternoon?

Thankfully, things aren't quite that bad. While it is true that it is essential when motivating to consider the very personal needs of the individual, it is also possible to define a set of practices that will work across the population, provided that you are prepared to establish just which elements an individual needs and the particular way of meeting those needs that fits best. It's a bit like running a clothes shop. The traditional, interchangeable component view says that you only need stock one size and style of each type of garment (and we aren't talking stretch material here). On the other hand, the sensible response isn't to design a whole new type of garment for each person. Whether you make-to-measure or sell off-the-peg, you will have the standard set of products like shirts, trousers, skirts and dresses.

One approach to tailored motivation is the Maslow hierarchy developed by Abraham Maslow. This provides a five-tier view of the factors that motivate people. Maslow's theory was that once one tier was satisfied it ceases to be a motivator and we move up to the next tier. The five stages are basic physiological needs, safety from fear, social needs, appreciation and pecking order, and realizing your potential. While Maslow's sequence seems much too structured for reality, these five elements all contribute to an individual's need for motivation, and at any one time an individual is likely to be more in need of certain elements – being in tune with this requirement can help a lot.

A RELATIONSHIP

The need to choose an appropriate approach to motivation of an individual implies having a relationship with him or her. You need to know the individual to best be able to motivate him or her. This doesn't mean you have to be drinking buddies or soul mates – just that knowing the individual is an essential to tailoring the motivation to fit. Inevitably, then, motivation is particularly difficult when you have just moved into a new job. You don't know the people around you; there is suspicion from all sides. If you are at an early stage in a job, building these relationships – with your staff, your peers, your superiors – is an essential step towards making individual motivation possible. This is why you will quite often see social activities as part of the exercises – not just because the social activity can be a motivation in itself, but also because it gives you an opportunity to build a relationship and open the door to more focused individual motivation. As that relationship builds, you can see which type of motivation is best suited at the moment (needs aren't static, they will change over time). Although there is actually a spectrum of styles of motivation, they can broadly be described as coaching, counselling, transforming and mentoring.

COACHING

All the ways you can motivate an individual are about enhancing performance and developing job satisfaction, but coaching takes the specific approach of bringing on an under-performer or helping someone who simply hasn't got the experience to do a job well. To be a great coach you don't have to be able to do the job yourself, but you do have to have an understanding of what it is about. The 1990s' fad for general-purpose managers (once more ignoring the individual) overlooked this benefit of having expertise in your business area.

The coach has to be aware of the requirements of the job and must be able to assess what is lacking in the individual. It may be a matter of training or practical experience. It may be that there are particular aspects of the role of the individual that need bringing on. It may also be that the individual is attempting a role or task that he or she is totally unsuited for. While this can sometimes be developmental as a one-off experience, the coach needs to be able to say that enough is enough and direct the individual away from this area. Here motivational skills rest in identifying other positive directions, so the individual is encouraged into a positive alternative use of his or her time, rather than being told that he or she is incapable of doing the original task.

A particular distinction the coach has to make is between stretch and over-stretch. Everyone benefits from being stretched. Often failure is the only route to success. There are many tasks that can only be achieved well after repeated, sometimes painful, failure. To maintain motivation the coach has to keep the individual aware of what is happening – that he or she is undergoing a learning process where failure is an inevitable step along the way, rather than hitting an absolute barrier. However, everyone has limits. These will change over time, but at any one point, the coach has to be sensitive to the individual's break points and not push beyond them.

COUNSELLING

Coaching generally assumes there is some skill or experience missing from the individual's performance. Sometimes all that is missing is self-esteem. The sheer belief in 'self' that can allow an individual to soar. Some individuals come with a natural self-confidence that carries them through, meaning they can take on a new role and act as if they were born for it. Others will be hesitant, either because they have a low opinion of themselves in general, or because they 'know' that they can't do this particular task.

When counselling someone who believes themselves incapable of the task, it is important to understand why they think this. It is often the case when an individual has less academic qualification than their peers, or is very new to a job while surrounded by experts. The aim is not to make the person over-confident, and hence derided by their peers, but to give them the confidence to try (and potentially try several times in the face of failure).

Often an early step to counselling can be to look objectively at the causes of low self-esteem. If the problem is lack of qualifications, discuss how limited the practical application of the qualifications actually is (almost always the case with higher education), and emphasize the benefits of real experience. If, on the other hand, the problem centres around being a very inexperienced person in an experienced crowd, emphasize how a fresh point of view can bring benefit to those who have been doing things 'the way we do it' so long that they can't see how things can be done better.

Watch out for the influence of others when counselling. I once had a very talented person working for me who was moving from a largely administrative job to a technical one. She felt intimidated by some of the others in her team, especially her team leader. He was not at all sure of her abilities, thinking she had got the job on her customer service skills, while he wanted to be sure of her technical ability. This initial reaction from the team leader had a negative effect on her self-esteem. However, when she had some achievements under her belt, a positive reaction from the same team leader was highly motivational – she had succeeded despite his concerns. It would have made it easier if he had taken an unbiased stance at the beginning, but his change of heart helped in the end.

TRANSFORMING

Like it or not, some tasks are boring and unattractive. They are naturally demotivating. It can also be the case that individuals bring an external problem into the workplace that can undermine any natural enthusiasm for the job. In such circumstances, the motivational role is one of identifying the problems and fixing them. This is a lesson from leadership – where a manager's role is often seen as making sure the staff do the right things – one of the leader's main tasks is getting the obstacles out of the way so that staff can get on with the real work.

Where the problem is centred on the job in hand, it is often within your capability to make changes which will transform the attitude to the task. Here motivation can take a wide range of forms. It might involve restructuring the task. A classic example would be moving from the soul-destroying repetition of undertaking a single action to involvement in the whole process of constructing a part or assembly. Such a change of direction gets better buy-in and results in better quality output. Similarly, other repetitious tasks can be varied by interlacing a range of activities.

Equally, motivation might involve special incentives. If there is no way to break up the tediousness of the task, find ways to add a side attraction. Extra pay at the end of the week or month aren't particularly good for this, as they are invisible and distant. Special incentives need to be obvious and immediate. Perhaps a prize for the day's best performance, or even a lottery with entries dependent on the products of the task. When we want children to undertake a task they don't enjoy, we try to turn it into a game to motivate them. A similar approach can work just as well with adults. If you can overcome the long-standing fear most companies have of employees actually enjoying themselves, you have a chance of ramping-up motivation on these unpopular tasks. This sort of approach can even help in the not uncommon position of motivating upwards, getting your boss to undertake something he or she doesn't particularly enjoy, like authorizing your expenses claim.

Sometimes the demotivating factor is external to work. You might feel that it isn't your place to get involved. After all you are a manager (or team leader, or whatever), not a social worker. Yet the fact is that leaving a festering problem outside the workplace isn't helpful to either of you. Counselling in such circumstances requires tact and care. The temptation might be to hand over to some professional counsellor, like a human resources professional if your company has one, but it is often not the right answer. The message this may give to the individual is that you don't really care yourself, so you are handing it over to HR. Instead, it is best to try to handle it yourself, supported discretely by HR if necessary.

You are unlikely to be the one who actually sorts out the problem in this circumstance. Unless it is a simple case of needing to write a letter from a position of authority, the chances are it is only the individual who can untangle things. But your positive support can be extremely beneficial, producing a lasting motivational factor.

MENTORING

Probably the hardest individual motivation is dealing with the high-performer, someone who is already doing the job well. So why bother to motivate them at all? In part because of retention. Just because someone does a job superbly well, it doesn't mean that they want to stay in it. They are susceptible to outside lures that makes positive motivation to stay a real benefit for the company. Also, however good they are, it doesn't mean that they can't be motivated to do more. The true high-performer doesn't work at 10 per cent above the average, but hundreds of per cent. Fine tuning reaps significant rewards.

There's another factor to motivating the high-performer, too, which paradoxically conflicts with the first argument. It may be that you need to motivate them out of their present job into something bigger and better. This is a difficult one for those who see motivation as only being about getting the most out of a resource – how can encouraging someone to leave their job do this? A major reason has to be concern for the individual – you should want them to go on to something better, just as you would your child, even if it hurts when they leave the home. However, there are less altruistic motives, too. Keep a high-performer down and eventually they will turn on you, becoming more and more destructive and devious. Worse still, a true high-performer will eventually escape, and may end up as your boss or your key customer. Would you rather be remembered as the person who gave them their big break, or the one who held them back?

Achieving motivation in this type of situation involves a role that may sound rather like coaching, but is actually quite different – mentoring. Mentoring doesn't put you in a position of authority, or even necessarily of expertise. As a mentor you are a sounding board for the individual's ideas and thoughts. You give them a chance to think things through with an intelligent audience. You can suggest different ways of going forward and ways of assessing those opportunities. You can even say what you would do in such circumstances. But in the end, your role is as an unthreatening, trusted person to discuss options with. This can be a highly satisfying role for you, and will be greatly valued by the individual. You may even end up in a mutual mentoring relationship, although you often find that your own mentors are different from those for whom you provide mentoring.

AVOIDING DEMOTIVATION

Motivating a person is not just about enhancing the positive – often it is about removing the negative. Whatever the positive needs of the individual, there are dangers of demotivation from sources that are common to everyone. In fact, a number of common factors that are often regarded as motivational actually aren't. Instead, they are elements which will demotivate if absent. A classic example is a good level of pay. Despite the gut reaction, paying people above the odds does not motivate them to do better – this is borne out by study after study. However, not paying people enough is a powerful demotivator. Pay isn't a motivational factor, it's a demotivation suppressor. These tranquilizers of the negative are sometimes referred to as hygiene factors, a term devised by psychologist Frederick Herzberg, but I find this term confusing and worryingly medical sounding.

The frightening thing once you start to look at which factors actually motivate and which just suppress demotivation, is that almost all the traditional ways that companies use to reward their staff are not motivational. Options like salary and perks, working conditions, job security and seniority all fall into the tranquilizer class. Much more motivational are actually achieving something (an outcome many bureaucracies seem devised to avoid), recognition, having true responsibility (not the same thing at all as seniority), having somewhere to go – the realistic potential to go further, and doing something interesting. Is it any wonder that motivation is a problem in many businesses? We've got our priorities skewed. Not upside down, because we still need to tranquilize the demotivators before we can get on with the positive, but certainly skewed the wrong way.

3

TEAM SPIRIT

WHAT IS A TEAM?

If the business world still hasn't really got a handle on the individual, it can hardly be said to have ignored the team. Teams have been fundamental to the business approach of the last 20 years of the 20th century and don't show any signs of disappearing in the 21st. You only have to compare the implied praise or criticism in the comments 'She's a real team player' and 'He's a bit of a loner' – we all know that teams are good. Yet knowing that something is good is not the same thing as understanding it, or being able to make it work. Pulling a team together to succeed is a complex activity. You are dealing with a group of individuals, with individual needs, yet it's not possible to take such a specific line as it is in a one-to-one situation. Having a broad understanding of how the individuals in the team will work together is essential. Most important of all is making the aims of the team something each member strives for, bringing synergy to their individual efforts.

It's worth taking a few moments first, though, just thinking about what a team is. A team is a minimum of two people working together towards shared goals. It may involve similar people working in parallel, where the team benefits are mostly about minimizing costs by sharing information and resources. Most white-collar teams are designed to produce synergy – bringing together complimentary skills to provide an outcome that is equal to more than the sum of the parts. This synergy derives from the interplay of thoughts and the ability to work together on a challenge rather than sequentially. The power of a team is in part down to the nature of knowledge. It is not simply an accumulation of information, but the mental structures needed to use that information – a team has a richer mental structure and a deeper pool of information with which to work.

WORKING TOGETHER... AND NOT

If a team is to gain those benefits of synergy it needs to be able to interact smoothly. This is often illustrated by using the image of well-oiled cogs in a machine, or a sporting team – but neither presents the ideal image. A business team is much more like a living organism. It needs the basics of survival, which are similar to a machine – the fuel of appropriate tasks and the internal communications, to make teamwork possible, but it also needs growth and fun. Growth, not in the sense of growing a team larger (the empire builder does not make a good team leader), but constantly growing in capabilities – a learning team. Fun, because a team thrives on positive interaction, which implies a fun atmosphere.

Part of making a team work together well is about providing all those essentials. Appropriate tasks – setting a team tasks that are achievable, but stretching. Internal communications – if a team can't be physically co-located it needs superb communications support across the whole spectrum. Growth – regular courses and reading, always pushing the boundaries of the team's capabilities. And fun – opportunities for social interaction and a working environment where fun isn't frowned on. It also helps to have an understanding of team roles. Different individuals, with different psychological profiles, will take on different roles in the team and will interact with other members of the team in different ways. This isn't the place to go into profiles in any depth, but the use of a recognized test, like Myers Briggs or the Insights Colour Wheel, can provide a valuable understanding of how a team will work together, and can give team members assistance in making it work.

The almost universal support for the team approach has resulted in one unexpected demotivating factor, which is rarely mentioned in the literature. Teams are not creative. This sounds like heresy. We all know the valuable innovation that comes from a team throwing an idea around, combining different inputs and building on them. The fact remains, though, that teams are not creative. The old joke about a camel being a horse designed by committee is based on fact. When you look at the evidence, it is the individual that creates ideas, while teams are good at refining, combining and enhancing them. Edward de Bono has argued that this is why the UK has produced so many new inventions, while the USA has made money out of them – the UK has more of a tradition of the (quite possibly eccentric) individual, while the USA has had a longer love affair with the team.

The lesson this provides for team motivation is that we need to give individuals, especially creative individuals, the space to get away from the team to hatch ideas, but to ensure that they also are encouraged to work with the team to develop and combine ideas. There are few more frustrating and demotivating factors for a creative individual than to force him or her into 'teamthink' at a point where a new idea is emerging. The keys are to make space for individual thought available (if you have an open-plan team room there should also be a room where individuals can lock themselves away), and to make sure that the role of the team is understood. To put across the message that while it is essential to be part of the team, it is equally important to give the other members of the team the space they need, when they need it.

TEAM GOALS

An important step towards understanding teams and making them work is having clear goals. This doesn't have to involve a formal system of cascading mission and goals and objectives and tasks – it can be as simple as a regularly revised list of bullet points tacked up on the wall. The important thing about team goals is that they are visible, understood and bought into. Failure in any of these requirements can demotivate and reduce the team's effectiveness.

Buy-in is an essential from a motivational viewpoint. If individuals in the team don't support the goals, they will undermine the motivation of the whole team. It's worth making sure that individuals aren't just giving lip service to the goals but actually believe that they are worthwhile. One way to increase buy-in is to make sure that the team members have an input to the goals. They should not expect to say 'This goal is rubbish', but they should have a sympathetic hearing if they say 'Why don't we change this goal like this, it will improve it?'

Part of the process of confirming buy-in should be testing understanding. You can't be fully behind goals you don't understand. Misunderstanding can lead to friction between team members, a powerful blockage to motivation. It is only a shared understanding between team members that will bring the goals alive.

Visibility has two aspects. The goals need to be visible to the team members. This allows them to compare their activities against the goals, to check that what they are doing has appropriate value. The goals should also be visible to people outside the team, so they can be aware of what the team is trying to achieve. This will motivate the team to perform better (provided the goals are appropriate and stretching) and will encourage others to support them.

TEAM BLOCKAGES

There are a number of circumstances and problems that can block a team's effectiveness and reduce its motivation. We have already seen the possibilities of misunderstandings within the team and of poorly understood goals. Other contributory factors can be lack of energy or tunnel vision, physical comfort, security, esteem and development.

The first two problems can be overcome with appropriate team exercises. They are covered in the companion volume *Instant Teamwork* (see Chapter 6 for more details). A strong team can work in physically unappealing surroundings and still be highly motivated. A team that is lacking in motivation will still fail despite a beautiful office. Yet some aspects of location can have an effect on motivation. Bad lighting, poor air-conditioning, cramped space can all reduced motivation. Bearing in mind that office space is very much 'home territory', it is not surprising that external changes also come across badly. Frequently enforced moves of office (implying low esteem), rigid control over décor and other commandments from on high can easily demotivate.

Within a team, office space can also result in internal strife. Simple matters, like who sits nearest the window, can be blown up out of all proportion – take office space seriously. In terms of esteem and development, you can almost treat a team as if it were an individual. A team expects recognition for what it achieves and the opportunity to develop and grow (not necessarily in size). Some companies have reward schemes with a performance pay component for team performance, but few recognize the strength of feeling that attaches to how a team is regarded by others in the company. There is a big opportunity here, both for motivation and demotivation – the choice is yours.

INSIDE OUT, NOT OUTSIDE IN

There's a world of difference between the phrases 'you are a team' and 'we are a team'. Teams are almost impossible to motivate from the outside. Most of the motivation has to come from within. Demotivation, on the other hand, can come in very easily from the outside – it's a one-way barrier. That's not to say that motivating factors can't be initiated from the outside. If your director gives your team an award it will have a motivating effect, but most of the motivation will come from the reaction within the team. This means that any recognition for a team ought to have a team flavour to it. If an individual gets a glowing write-up in the in-house magazine it will have a big impact. For a team it will be less effective. However, if the team goes out for a meal on the boss, even though the visibility level of the recognition is much lower, it will have a big impact, because it is a team event and gives the team a chance to build on the morale boost.

If you want to bring a team on, it is important that the team regards you as 'one of us' not 'one of them'. Unfortunately, this isn't as simple as just stating the fact. When a large company's chief executive tells the staff that 'We're all one big team' he might be trying to achieve this sense of joint purpose and buy-in, but it simply doesn't work. Teams form by interaction, not by organizational structure. You have to earn your position in the team before you will be 'one of us' – and that goes for everyone, even the chief executive. This doesn't mean you have to do one of the 'ordinary' jobs on the team, but that the team members have to consider your contribution relevant and meaningful.

MOTIVATING THE TEAM

When looking at the motivation of the team, you are working at two levels. The individual considerations still apply, but there are team factors as well. Teams still have demotivational tranquilizers and motivational uppers, but the flavour is rather different. Elements like pay and seniority disappear from the negatives to be suppressed, while factors like working conditions often increase in importance. As already discussed, positive motivational factors, which can be appreciated by the team *as a team*, have a greater impact than motivators that apply to each individual in the team as individuals.

Although all the roles of coaching, counselling, transforming and mentoring that applied to individuals can also be applied to the team, again there is a different weighting. Counselling may still be about self-esteem (there is a pecking order to teams, and some will consider themselves of low importance), but it is often about internal relationships. As we saw in *Team blockages* above, relationship problems can cripple the working of a team, destroying its motivation from within. The team motivator needs to be a good relationship counsellor. But the team also adds a fifth motivational role – leading.

This isn't the book to go into the details of leadership (see Chapter 6 for more details of the companion volume *Instant Leadership*), but the nature of the leadership provided is central to the motivation of a team. Leadership, rather than management, is the key word. If you accept the crude distinction between leadership and management – that good leaders provide a combination of very stretching goals with high support, while good managers provide well-defined tasks with excellent monitoring – leadership is an inevitable requirement for team motivation. A leader will feel part of the team, even though setting the direction. A leader will provide clear principles and make sure everyone understands exactly what their priorities are – but will let the team get on with getting something done. A leader will be focused on outputs – what is delivered by when, not inputs – who works the right hours wearing the right suit. I would go so far as to say that you can't effectively motivate a team without good leadership.

4

LARGE SCALE

BIG GROUPS

Whatever reason a large group of people has for getting together – a conference, an in-house training day, a company forum – there is likely to be a mix of attitudes from the enthusiastic to the cynical. Without the right motivation, a huge investment in time is likely to be wasted. As always with motivation it's not a one-way thing either. The people attending the event, or forming part of the body, will get much more out of it if they are properly motivated. But getting such a group motivated takes a broader brush approach than a team – it's less personal, more oriented to the underlying influences that motivate everyone. That isn't to say that we've returned to the picture of inter-changeable components. Members of a large group are still individuals, and it's often the input of one or more individuals that will influence the motivation of the group as a whole. There is no magic super-psychology, like Isaac Asimov's fictional psycho-history that allows us to consider a large group as a single complex entity. Yet there are considerations which make them practical to deal with.

WHY ARE THEY HERE?

The reasons for attending a large group are varied, but they fall broadly into four categories. Knowing the type of attendee you have at a large group session can influence your approach to motivation.

Some attendees will be there because they have been sent. They wouldn't choose to be present, but their boss has told them to be, or there's a company-wide edict. Often they will feel that the session is a waste of time that would be better spent on their normal working activities. Motivating people like this is particularly hard – it requires a lot of effort, but without getting them on-board they are likely to be disruptive and uncooperative.

Some attendees may simply be there for a break. Because it's a great excuse not to work. This can sound harsher than it is – we all need to get away from things occasionally, and a large group session might be a good opportunity to recharge the batteries. Such people may never get fully behind your intentions, but will generally be easy to motivate as they have already achieved what they wanted.

A third type of attendee has a specific agenda. They know exactly what they want to get out of the session. Nothing else will do. If you are pretty close to their require-ment motivation will not be an issue, but anything that strays away from it (and such a closed picture is fairly unlikely to match a whole session) will be ignored, some-times in a very obvious way. In those circumstances this group are just as much of a challenge as those who have been sent involuntarily.

The final type has a general passion for learning and developing. It doesn't really matter what the subject is as long as they are growing. The only motivational danger with this group is if your session doesn't have enough content. If it is all froth and no substance the people in this group will start getting itchy feet, but otherwise they are easy to please.

WHY DO YOU WANT THEM THERE?

Just as there are a small number of reasons for attending a session, there are a small number of reasons for organizing them. You might want to get information across, you might be engaging in training, or simply trying to influence the mood of a group. Although there are plenty of other labels attached, these three categories cover most large sessions. It's quite possible, of course, for a session to switch between categories during the event. For instance, a departmental awayday may start with information on the company, move on to a training session on a new way of working and end up with cheerleading to send the department out on a high. Even so, the different sections have different requirements.

INFORMING

In an information session you want the attendees to be motivated to listen to your message and to take it away in a form that will be remembered and used appropriately. Classic informing sessions are management briefings and press conferences. Some of the motivational factors also apply to the other categories. I have attended so many events (especially press events) where you are made to wait around for at least half an hour after the published start time, often kept out of the auditorium where the event is about to take place. This is not a good start to encourage constructive listening.

Once into the session, good use of support media (to illustrate rather than to be flashy for the sake of it) and an engaging speaking style make a lot of difference. If your presenter drones unmercifully, usually talking incomprehensible jargon, you will have lost your audience in minutes. Make sure you have a decent speaker, and a run-through of the presentation in advance to catch glitches.

A great speaker, or an exciting video, can put across a message very effectively without anything else. Yet the retention capabilities of the brain will still start to limit what is taken in unless specific steps are taken. One requirement is frequent breaks, carving up the message into manageable chunks (it is also pretty demotivating if you are desperate to get to the bathroom). Another requirement for retention is the ability to revisit the input. For this reason, a good way to motivate the attendees to revise your information is to give them an interesting way of doing it. This might mean just having a handout of the slides, but this is the bare minimum (and an awful lot of packs of handouts spend the rest of their life on the shelf, never being looked at again).

Consider other, more fun ways to carry the message home. Can you put it on a laminated card to go in their personal organizers? Can you give away a book that puts across the message? Real books always have more impact than handouts. Can you give them the information to take away in a different medium? Beware, by the way, of the illusion that high-tech is necessarily the answer. Although, for instance, you can build a very fancy CD-ROM with your message presented as a dramatic multimedia presentation, a lot of people won't look at it. They might not have drives or, like me, they may be swamped with CD-ROMs from different sources and never get round to doing anything with your masterpiece.

Sometimes you can get more benefit from a more tangential approach. Give them something that is attractive in its own right that will remind them of your message. It might be a bag or a T-shirt with an appropriate message. It could be a penknife or practically any other gift that can have a few words printed on it. The important thing, though, is to judge your audience and the kind of give-away that is likely to appeal.

TRAINING

In a sense, training is a special case of informing, but it is different enough to treat independently. For our purposes the difference in a training session, whether it's a seminar or a workshop or a conventional training course, is the complexity of the message that has to be got across. Usually it will be more detailed and will often involve practical experience rather than just being talked at.

All of the motivational tricks that apply to informing can be brought over into training too, but some extra ones apply. Making the exercises enjoyable, and ensuring that the content is relevant to the training requirement are essential. Generally, hands-on experience in training is particularly motivational, although it can have a negative effect if it is very exposed – most people don't like their learning mistakes to be viewed by everyone. Because training often involves breaking the group into small teams, many of the team aspects of motivation discussed in the previous chapter apply here, too.

Although it is potentially a problem in all three forms of group exercise, training is particularly susceptible to boredom. There is a phenomenon where regular attendees of training sessions become fed up with the format. I have seen groups rebel because they had had enough of being broken up into syndicate sessions, who then reported back to the full group – they wanted something different. Bear this in mind. If you do want to break up into teams, make them as different as possible. If you do want reporting back, don't make it a case of everyone giving a two-minute presentation, go for something outrageously different. This is particularly important if you are running a session over several days and want to keep the motivation level up.

CHEERLEADING

A cheerleading session has pure motivation as its prime goal. You don't want to send people away informed or trained, but with a warm glow about your subject. A classic cheerleading event is a sales conference, where the salespeople (delicate flowers one and all) are encouraged and led on by the successes of others. Less obvious, but equally cheerleading in nature, are celebrations. It might be your annual company barbecue, your Christmas party or a meal to celebrate completing a project – whichever, motivation is its *raison d'être*.

Motivating in a cheerleading session is usually blatant and works mostly at a gut level. Anything from actual cheerleaders to special effects, videos, lavish prizes and razzmatazz can contribute to a cheerleading session. This is fine as long as it is done in a style that is appropriate for the group taking part, and isn't seen as over-costly or celebration in a time of difficulty. Otherwise, there could well be problems as discussed in *Avoiding farce* below.

DIFFUSE GROUPS

Perhaps the hardest large groups to motivate are diffuse groups, where the individuals involved may not even realize that they are members of a group. Consider all the potential customers for your products and services. Not the customers you've already got, but the ones you might have in the future (though, of course, your existing customers are a group, too). They are never going to be together in the same location. Many of the traditional motivating techniques are simply irrelevant. At this level, motivation becomes more aligned with marketing than conventional interpersonal skills. Yet all the lessons from the different types of grouping described above are still likely to be valuable.

GETTING THE BANDWAGON ROLLING

An unfairly large part of the motivational opportunity with a large group rests in the first few minutes of its existence. Luckily, through the flow of a day there are usually several 'first few minutes' – after the group has been broken up and reformed, after breaks and meals. Setting the right tone in those first few minutes can make a lot of difference to motivation. One contributory factor has already been mentioned – getting started promptly. It is also very valuable to get started with a bang. Resist the temptation to drone through a summary of the day, and safety regulations and how to find the toilets. Getting the group into a positive frame of mind, perhaps using one of the exercises described in *Instant Teamwork* (see Chapter 6) is a much better starting point. Similarly, a very short multimedia presentation can help to introduce a positive, anticipatory state. Be intensely aware of the opportunities those first few minutes present.

AVOIDING FARCE

When you are dealing with large groups, you are working at a particularly emotional level. Like any serious drama, you have to tread carefully to avoid flipping into farce. This is a particular danger if those attempting to put across the motivational message are more serious about it than those receiving the message. Grand spectacular can have superb results, but misjudged messages can have the opposite effect.

A wonderful case study is provided by the major relaunch international airline British Airways undertook in the 1980s. With the memory of being a nationalized company still around, BA took a bold step in transforming the company, highlighted by a striking new livery. This was launched in a stunning show. The whole audience was on a mobile platform that first raised to an upper level for a speech by the senior executives, then returned to the lower level for a light show that ended with the audience's platform moving towards the screens. As they did, the screens fell away and there, spotlighted through the smoke, was a model plane in the new livery, revolving on a turntable. It took a few seconds to realize the scale of the event – this wasn't a model, it was an actual 737 jet. This event took the breath away and was genuinely motivational. (This shouldn't be confused with the livery change BA undertook in the 1990s which received much flak from the press and public, and was spectacularly demotivational.)

This event worked because of the sheer scale and drama, and because the message fitted. However, dressing up an unconvincing message with excessive razzmatazz can have the reverse effect to that intended. Those attending can go away thinking 'What a waste of money – so what?' This can be the case where an expensive presentation is used to launch a cost-cutting exercise, but more typically it happens when there is no belief among the group that those putting across the message really mean it, or that they can deliver on the promise. This response is often seen in political events. Large-scale glitz works superbly when it is supporting a strong message – as smoke and mirrors to conceal an absence of message it is an effective (and expensive) demotivator.

5

THE EXERCISES

5.1 | *It's catching*

Preparation None.
Running time 10 minutes.
Resources Notepad.
Frequency Once.

The whole aim of this book is to help you to motivate other people. One of the best tips on motivation is noticing that it is infectious. If you are genuinely motivated in what you are doing, if it gives you real satisfaction and you are totally committed to it, it will rub off on those around you.

This isn't the place to discuss self-motivation and assertiveness in any detail. However, spending a few minutes looking at your own motivation will generate significant benefits. Try out the *Portfolio matching* (5.26) exercise on yourself. Note down how motivated you are in the areas where you are trying to motivate others. Make sure you have that essential buy-in and enthusiasm. With it, you will succeed in motivating others.

Feedback   The question arises, what happens if you aren't motivated yourself? Apart from looking at the possibilities of self-motivation, you have a number of options. Discuss it with those who have the opportunity to motivate you. Look at why you aren't motivated and see if you can remove the obstacles. If all else fails, find a way of doing something else. You can only keep up a facade of motivation for so long, and demotivation is even more infectious than motivation. You owe it to yourself to be doing something that excites you.

Outcome   This is one of the most powerful techniques available in motivation. We aren't all capable of generating charisma, but everyone can provide enthusiasm and interest. This will communicate itself to others.

Variations   This technique works across the whole spectrum of audiences, from individuals to huge groups. It is not an option.

Individual	✪✪✪✪
Team	✪✪✪✪
Group	✪✪✪✪
Fun	✪✪✪✪

5.2 | *Somewhere to go*

Preparation None.
Running time 10 minutes.
Resources None.
Frequency Occasional.

We are all driven by the desire to get somewhere. The destination differs wildly from person to person and often is not clear, but the need is there. If you want someone to be motivated in their job, they need to feel that they have somewhere to go – that they aren't in a dead-end job. Actually getting advancement is, of course, an effective source of motivation, but most long-term value comes from the feeling that there is somewhere to go, and there is a realistic opportunity of getting there. After all, job changes will rarely happen more than once every few years, but opportunities to use the motivational power of possible future advancement occur every day.

Take a few minutes to look at the possibilities for advancement with someone you'd like to motivate. It's important to be realistic about timescales and not to raise false hopes in this process. If you find that there aren't enough prospects within a timescale that is meaningful for the individual, arrange a second session, before which you can come up with something helpful. If you can't find anything, perhaps this is a hint that you ought to help this person to look for opportunities outside your company. Better that than keep them inside, disillusioned and bitter.

Feedback   The easy mistake with this technique is to assume that advancement means promotion. Increasingly with flatter organizations, promotion is less common. Instead, advancement can also be seen as taking on new roles – but they should be clear-cut new roles, with new challenges and different prospects. A useful precursor to looking at advancement possibilities is to do the exercise *Portfolio matching* (5.26). This will give both of you a better picture of the advancement that is most likely to motivate.

Outcome   Advancement within the company is a personal goal for almost everyone. By making it explicit it becomes a powerful motivator – provided reality makes a reasonable match to expectations.

Variations   None.

Individual	✪✪✪✪
Team	✪
Group	✪
Fun	✪✪

5.3 | *Demolishing demotivators*

Preparation None.
Running time 15 minutes.
Resources None.
Frequency Occasional.

This book concentrates largely on positive motivation, but it is worth considering occasionally the potential demotivators – the factors that don't contribute much positive motivation, but will certainly prove problematic if handled wrongly.

A handy approach is to draw up a table of the factors and revisit them occasionally. Against each factor, note how you think you do against normal expectation and look for a couple of points where you can make an improvement.

Key factors here are pay (and associated benefits), the general conditions of employment, the working environment and equipment, perceived job security, level of authority and autonomy (and associated degree of supervision) and company bureaucracy – see *Banishing bureaucracy* (5.70) for more on this insidious factor.

Feedback Don't ignore one of these killer factors just because you don't think you can influence it directly. If there is active demotivation, you need to do something about it – in fact, the very fact that you are taking notice can help a lot. Can you get round the system (eg in dealing with bureaucracy) or plead a special case? Can you get involved in future changes of approach?

In considering demotivating factors, don't be concerned that you are bringing together apparently insignificant factors with very important ones. If someone can never find a place to park when they arrive at work, it can be much more demotivating than knowing that they are paid 2 per cent below the median salary for their job. Take a broader viewpoint.

Outcome These factors are the non-glamorous spadework of motivation, providing the foundations to build the more exciting possibilities like recognition and responsibility. Like all foundations, they are essential for effective progress.

Variations Because of the very subjective nature of some of these factors it is worth checking with the individuals involved just what they see as the biggest frustrations at the moment.

Individual	✪✪✪✪
Team	✪✪
Group	✪
Fun	✪✪

5.4 | *Publish and be damned*

Preparation None.
Running time 10 minutes.
Resources None.
Frequency Regular.

On a regular basis, spend a few minutes thinking of how you can use your company publications to improve motivation. Bear in mind that 'publications' covers a multitude of vehicles. It can be a company magazine or newspaper, departmental or team equivalents, bulletins, newsletters and increasingly the in-house version of the Internet, an intranet. Describing individual, team and company successes can be very positive for those involved, provided the publication is not seen as a vehicle for company whitewash and only ever carrying good news. Publications also give staff an opportunity to contribute letters and comments. Combine this with editorial action on comments to give the best motivational effect.

Feedback Publications traditionally have a low impact on motivation because they are bland and careful, putting across the company line. Consider starting a publication with an action-orientation that is slightly subversive in tone, giving a strong voice to the staff. Any publication that can be seen as 'ours' is much more likely to be read – and to provide motivation. It should not be allowed to be a simple 'moan sheet', which is anything but motivational – perhaps a good model would be the TV-consumer rights' programmes, where the goal is not to moan but to get a result.

Outcome Provided publications are action-orientated and not pure hype they will benefit motivation.

Variations A particular variant of the publication is the bulletin board. This could be a literal noticeboard, but is more likely to be an electronic one, like a Web discussion or a Lotus Notes database. To have motivational benefit, such a discussion needs to have regular management input, picking up concerns and responding to them. Because of the time constraints, such electronic publications are the best approach for large groups, although for sessions lasting more than a half day it is also possible to put together a paper publication, which may give more lasting impact.

Individual	✪✪✪✪
Team	✪✪✪✪
Group	✪✪✪
Fun	✪✪✪

5.5 | *Arrivals*

Preparation None.
Running time Five minutes.
Resources None.
Frequency Regular.

There's something very motivating about arriving. If you are always on the road, but never get anywhere it can be very depressing. All too often work involves projects with long timescales, or even no completion date because it's a task that continues forever.

To introduce a motivating element, make sure that there are regular arrivals for individuals and teams. When considering a project, look for milestones along the way. When considering an endless project, find measures that can give completion for a particular section. How you mark arrivals can vary enormously, both on the type of work involved and the people. At one extreme it can be simply ticking a box. At the other it can be the sort of event described in *Celebration time* (5.41). The important thing is that there are arrivals, which the individuals involved recognize as worthwhile.

Feedback I've often used the example of electronic commerce firm Entranet, where the managing director tries to make sure that there's an arrival every day. It might be an article about them in a newspaper, or the delivery of a new drinks machine, or the completion of a major project, but there is some arrival. Some people feel that this is too often, and too mechanical. There is a danger that arrival becomes routine, but that needn't be the case if it is handled properly. For many it might be more appropriate to have a couple of arrivals a week, but this does not in any way invalidate the daily arrival as a worthy model.

Outcome Arrivals are diluted by distance, which is why they are not particularly effective at a large group level. But made personal, or relevant to a team that the individual associates strongly with, they can be a great, low-effort motivator.

Variations Try starting with one a week – everyone ought to be able to manage this level.

Individual	✪✪✪✪
Team	✪✪✪
Group	✪✪
Fun	✪✪✪

5.6 | *Risk and failure*

Preparation Failure.
Running time 10 minutes.
Resources None.
Frequency Regular.

Your attitude to failure can have a key effect on motivation. Too often in corporate culture, particularly a US-based culture, failure is seen as an ineradicable black mark. Yet all great thinkers sing the praise of failure – fast failure. The desirable approach is to fail fast, learn fast and put the lesson into practice.

The only way to avoid risk is to stick to a totally known procedure in a totally known environment. As all totally known environments are artificial, this has limited application to business. There will be risk; there will be failure. When something goes wrong, take a few minutes with those involved to say 'What went wrong – how can we do better in the future?' This is not a blame-finding exercise, but positive learning.

Feedback The Total Quality Management (TQM) movement has many positive attributes, but it gives entirely the wrong impression about failure. The goal of TQM is zero failure – which is fine in a repetitive process. It's a goal for a production line, not a flexible, evolutionary, constantly changing environment. Keep TQM where it belongs.

The enthusiasm for failure should not blind you to the occasional person who won't learn lessons (see *Firm but fair*, 5.40). Nor does it mean you should take wild risks because you are generating helpful failures. Risk should be calculated, but once the risk has been taken, look forward not backward.

Outcome Fear of being seen to fail is a huge demotivator in many large companies. It results in timid decision-taking and minimal innovation. This isn't acceptable in a time of rapid change – if this culture can be modified, and you can do your bit, there will be a huge impact on both motivation and effectiveness.

Variations Large meetings and training sessions are a special case here. Because they are in an artificial environment you should generally minimize risk, unless you are involved in a creative exercise or learning about the benefits of failure.

Individual	✪✪✪✪
Team	✪✪✪
Group	✪
Fun	✪✪

5.7 | *Contributors*

Preparation None.
Running time Five minutes.
Resources None.
Frequency Regular.

To enhance motivation through contribution, consider this plan:

- Make it easy to contribute. One of the elements here might be scrapping your suggestion scheme (if that seems strange, see *Smashing the suggestion box*, 5.35).

- Treat contributions with respect, whoever they're from. Be prepared to give five minutes of your time to discuss them.

- Act quickly. This doesn't mean always doing what's suggested. But whether you implement the idea or have a good explanation of why you aren't, act.

Bear in mind that contributions aren't always ideas – it might just be doing something helpful without being asked – whatever, the contribution needs to be recognized.

Feedback This one's either catch-22 or a self-fulfilling prophecy. The more you take people's self-generated contributions seriously, the more motivated they will feel, and the more they will contribute. Similarly, the more you ignore contributions, the more they will be demotivated and cease to contribute. The difficulty that is sometimes faced is to reverse the spiral, especially when it is being enforced by demotivated middle managers. Whether trivial, or requiring a major overhaul of staff relations, it's worthwhile.

Outcome Another of the great win–wins: you can both enhance motivation, and directly improve productivity and new ideas for the company.

Variations Although primarily an individual and team technique, large groups involved in an interactive session will also quickly pick up mood and motivation from the way you handle suggestions and questions.

Individual	✪✪✪✪
Team	✪✪✪✪
Group	✪✪✪
Fun	✪✪

5.8 | *Eye eye*

Preparation None.
Running time Five minutes.
Resources A mirror.
Frequency Once.

Eye contact is a fundamental component in face-to-face motivation. Spend a couple of minutes on your own with a mirror. You will feel silly, but don't let it stop you. Before you start, produce a few keyword notes of a script, assuming that you were having to tell someone that they had performed well, but because of external circumstances they were going to have to do even more. Now deliver this message to yourself in the mirror. Try to keep good eye contact with yourself. This does not mean staring constantly into your eyes (this is off-putting – look away occasionally, but naturally), but make sure that you are looking into your eyes when you make your key points, and for most of the time.

Feedback After this exercise, try to be conscious of your eye contact when you are talking to people. Don't be tempted to look away when the message is bad. Poor eye contact means that you will be interpreted as being devious and not believing in what you are saying. You will be seen as being uncomfortable in their presence. Good eye contact reinforces the message and signals your commitment.

Outcome You can only motivate with visible sincerity. No matter how much you genuinely believe in your message, if your eyes say you don't, the message will not be believed. By enhancing your eye contact you will do wonders for your ability to motivate.

Variations Although described at an individual level, eye contact is also important when dealing with teams and groups. Here you will have to scan, trying to spread your eye contact across the group. This can seem artificial (for you) to begin with, but it does work. Watch a good speaker in action. Look also at other aspects of body language that can enhance motivation.

Individual	✪✪✪✪
Team	✪✪✪
Group	✪✪✪
Fun	✪✪

5.9 | *Tooling up*

Preparation Meeting with staff.
Running time 10 minutes.
Resources None.
Frequency Occasional.

Not having the right tools for the job is a common demotivating factor for professionals. Have irregular, short meetings with your staff. Ask them to come with a list of what is bad in the current environment. At the meeting, get this list prioritized. Then take the top couple of items and get estimated costs and benefits for them. If they make sense, make every effort to get them in place.

You won't get everything your staff want. Just because a salesperson feels that driving a Ferrari will get them closer to their sales target, you needn't rush out and buy one. But, equally, it is possible to overlook essentials. Particularly in a technical field, something which seems of little value to you may have a considerable impact on motivation. While you must weigh up solid costs and benefits, remember to include less tangible benefits in your assessment.

Feedback A good example is PCs for computer programmers. Programmers always want the fastest, best PCs. This is partly because they are posers, but it also has real benefit. Some elements of programming are particularly processor intensive. Repeated compiling can leave the expensive programmer twiddling his or her fingers most of the day. Not to upgrade a programmer's PC yearly is a false economy. Make sure, though, that they can quantify the benefit – and that they keep an old PC around to test their product on, as programmers who are only exposed to the latest machines get a false impression of what it's like to use their products.

Outcome Motivation frequently doesn't involve spending money, but sometimes you have to reach for the corporate chequebook. This is an example with very clear rewards, which are often ignored because we only count the cost and not the benefit.

Variations Do try to do this exercise in a meeting, because you can make use of the expertise of other staff members to shoot down suggestions based on personal inclination rather than general good.

Individual	✪✪✪✪
Team	✪✪✪✪
Group	✪✪
Fun	✪✪✪

5.10 | *Stretch but don't stress*

Preparation None.
Running time Five minutes.
Resources None.
Frequency Regular.

Very few people with an interest in their job want to be doing nothing, or performing tasks that they could complete in their sleep. There is something very valuable about being stretched. When thinking about the tasks people are doing, the messages they are being given – in any activity – ensure that as much as possible there is stretch incorporated into the content.

Have a regular stretch assessment for your staff (don't call it this; it sounds silly). Make sure that what they are doing is challenging – but possible. An element of stretch is essential – too much challenge becomes dangerous stress. Don't be afraid to ask people, but be aware that most people don't like to publicly define their limitations and may well be uncomfortable saying what is stretching until they are sure that the context isn't threatening. Stretching isn't necessarily about increasing volume – it is better if it's more responsibility, decision-making and depth of content rather than pure quantity.

Feedback Stretch is just as important when dealing with a large group as with an individual. If what you are talking about, or what they are undertaking, doesn't stretch them they are going to lose interest and switch off (or even go to sleep). The problem with dealing with a large group is defining what will stretch them, but not go over their heads. It is harder to assess than with an individual. Ideally, you should have some profile of those involved to be able to match to that reasonably well. If in doubt, though, get on-the-spot feedback (you may need to be quite assertive to get this out of a large group), and don't fall into the trap of underestimating them.

Outcome Stretch is another of the motivation all-round winners. Not only will you enhance motivation, but you are actually getting more out of your staff or out of the session the people are attending.

Variations None.

Individual	✪✪✪✪
Team	✪✪✪✪
Group	✪✪✪✪
Fun	✪✪✪

5.11 | *Gift aid*

Preparation None.
Running time 10 minutes.
Resources Budget.
Frequency Occasional.

It's generally accepted that an annual performance bonus and occasional one-off bonuses for outstanding work are good motivators. It's less well accepted that there should be a sizeable budget for such awards. Many companies only allow for a small amount – perhaps £100–£200 per head – which has negligible impact alongside a salary. Small bonuses can come both from company inertia and union suspicion that allowing more of the salary to be a performance-related bonus moves away from collective bargaining and puts the individual at the mercy of bad managers.

Whatever the reasoning, there is a way to improve the impact of a small bonus – don't give it. Instead, give each person due a bonus a gift, personally chosen to suit the individual. Yes, it's a real pain for the manager, but it gives it significantly more value. Properly chosen, the gift will seem much more worthwhile than the cash, because it adds a degree of opulence most people wouldn't normally bother with. £200 is not much when you see it as cash alongside an annual salary. But it's a lot for a watch or for dinner and a room at a hotel – the result being a gift that's really appreciated.

Feedback Don't fall into the trap of giving gift vouchers or a 'staff reward catalogue' to choose from. These are just a particularly weak form of money. The whole point of giving a gift rather than money is that it is personal and that it allows for more luxury than the individual would choose for themselves.

Outcome Gifts stretch a bonus well beyond its value. A small bonus can actually be demotivating – an equivalent gift has quite the reverse effect.

Variations If the bureaucracy in your company is such that giving a gift is not possible, consider allowing the individual to select the charity of their choice for the company to give the money to. Strangely, even though the individual gets less, this is more motivating than giving them a pitifully small bonus.

Individual	✪✪✪✪
Team	✪✪
Group	✪
Fun	✪✪✪

5.12 | *Do it themselves*

Preparation Individual meeting with staff.
Running time 10 minutes.
Resources None.
Frequency Once.

It is often the case that no one can motivate an individual as well as they can motivate themselves. Why not give their self-motivation a chance? Spend a few minutes with each individual. Get them to consider what it is that they really enjoy doing, both in and out of a work context. Help them to use these enjoyment factors to motivate themselves, ideally by directly incorporating them into their work or indirectly by giving themselves a target to reach, after which they can have a 'reward' of something they enjoy.

Although time management sounds to some like a lot of mechanistic rules, good time management is essential for self-motivation. It is almost impossible to manage your time without motivation in what you are doing. See Chapter 6 for some time management recommendations.

Feedback Self-motivation is something that writers like me are often asked about. 'How do you discipline yourself to sit down and work?' is a frequent question. Self-motivation is a mix of making sure you do plenty of what you like doing, survival (because if I don't do it I won't eat) and routine. Enabling your staff to build up their own routine (perhaps coming into work earlier than most or later than most), and maximizing their ability to make their working space personalized are both very helpful in self-motivation.

Outcome If you can get staff motivating themselves, you can't actually relax and not give it any consideration yourself, but it's certainly one of the most effective bits of delegation you are ever likely to do.

Variations Although this exercise is described as applying to an individual, you can also encourage a team to self-motivate by looking at the team as a whole and enabling individuals within the team to encourage each other.

Individual	✪✪✪✪
Team	✪✪✪
Group	✪
Fun	✪✪

5.13 | *Share and enjoy*

Preparation Investigate staff share schemes.
Running time 15 minutes.
Resources None.
Frequency Once.

This is a planning activity. Spend a few minutes looking into the potential of using shares and share options as a motivational reward for good performance. This is common practice for senior management and in high-tech and startup firms, but much less common for ordinary staff in many traditional firms. The potential benefits are high, because the individuals develop a greater interest in the performance of the company, and because there is an opportunity to make considerable rewards with less immediate impact on the company's finances. A further motivational benefit is that many stock options involve considerable anticipation, and it is often the case with motivational rewards that the anticipation has greater value than the actual reward.

Feedback A common argument against providing stock options for 'ordinary' staff is that they aren't interested in such things and/or don't understand. This simply won't do – the argument should be reworded that you haven't interested and informed them, and that you haven't explained the stock options properly. A more realistic argument as to why stock options aren't available more widely as a performance reward is that they are used as an old-fashioned status symbol, like a reserved car parking space – this simply isn't acceptable in a modern company, and certainly not one that is attempting to improve motivation.

Outcome Stock options are more powerful as a motivational and loyalty-buying incentive than cash – hence their popularity with senior management. They can be just as valuable with all staff.

Variations Few individuals have the authority to change the stock options available to staff, or to make changes in the company reward scheme. This activity is mostly about looking at what is possible. To get something done, you will probably have to lobby your human resources/personnel function and get other managers and directors involved in the change.

Individual	✪✪✪✪
Team	✪
Group	✪
Fun	✪✪✪

5.14 | *Understanding your style*

Preparation None.
Running time Five minutes.
Resources None.
Frequency Once.

When looking at motivation, your own management style will influence those you have to motivate. Tick the boxes below for the paired statements that match you best. Be honest!

Leadership

☐ 1. I can trust my staff.

☐ 2. The carrot is more effective than the stick.

☐ 3. I see myself as part of the team.

☐ 4. The successes of my team will reflect well on me.

☐ 5. My key role is to give my team a direction and support them in heading towards it.

☐ 6. I expect my staff to put forward ideas without prompting and to contribute to decision making.

Management

☐ 1. I need to monitor my staff closely.

☐ 2. Following the appropriate rules is an essential for discipline.

☐ 3. I need to distance myself from the team to keep roles clear.

☐ 4. My successes will reflect well on my team.

☐ 5. My key role is to give my team clear and specific objectives and to monitor achievement of them.

☐ 6. Leaders have to take key decisions on their own.

Feedback   Both the leadership and management styles are appropriate for different situations, but if your intention is to improve motivation, the leadership style is usually preferable. To get a much wider picture of leadership techniques see *Instant Leadership* (details in Chapter 6).

Outcome   Working on your management style can have a positive effect on the motivation of your staff – and often it is easier to change yourself than others.

Variations   None.

Individual	✪✪✪✪
Team	✪✪✪✪
Group	✪
Fun	✪✪

5.15 | *Meeting motivation*

Preparation Meeting.
Running time Five minutes.
Resources None.
Frequency Occasional.

Meetings should provide a real opportunity for motivation. Just sending someone to a meeting can be motivating as it implies that you value their input. Meetings give an opportunity for people to be heard and to feel that their input is being used. They can build mutual understanding and trust through shared values.

Good agenda management is important to make sure that meetings actually work in this way – and a strong chair may be needed to ensure that some individuals don't dominate the meeting and leave others demotivated. Every now and then think about the meetings you and your staff attend. Which should you drop? Which can you send someone else to in order to motivate them? You can also use meetings with the specific intent of motivation. Such meetings should be short, with good use of visual aids. There needs to be some good news to put across – extra sales, departmental performance, whatever – and the news needs to be of some relevance to those in the meeting. Be wary of using motivational meetings that are all cheerleading and no content. Sophisticated modern workers are rightly suspicious of such events and can actually be demotivated by them.

Feedback It's strange that so strong a motivational (and general business) tool as a meeting has such a bad reputation. Try asking people whether they need more meetings, or whether meetings come high up their list of what they like at work. On the whole they are considered necessary evils. A major reason for this is how meetings are misused. They over-run, they stray from the point, they can be self-perpetuating, they often have the wrong people present and no authority to actually do something… meetings are a bit of a nightmare. Good meeting control is an essential part of time management – see Chapter 6 for details of the companion *Instant Time Management*.

Outcome Meetings have a bad press, but it's all down to misuse. They can be a valuable motivational tool.

Variations None.

Individual	✪✪✪✪
Team	✪✪✪
Group	✪
Fun	✪✪

5.16 ***Perspective shift***

Preparation Meeting.
Running time 30 minutes.
Resources None.
Frequency Occasional.

In other activities we look at the way change can influence motivation both negatively (*Change control*, 5.32) and positively (*Change as motivator*, 5.49). A significant cushion to the negative and a boost to the chance to use the positive will come from engaging in a perspective shift. Like many motivational exercises, this is essentially one of communication. The old and still common world view was of careers as a steady progression through jobs, based on length of time in service. Most people would stay with a company (or even department) all their working lives – and what that company did would not change. Rules and procedures were there to be obeyed not questioned.

This old view was always a fiction, but never more so than now. Careers are becoming more non-linear and aptitude-based, with managers often younger than those they manage. Changes from department to department and company to company are frequent, with more people contracting out their skills. Loyalty is first to the individual themselves, then to their workgroup and only then to the company. It is more important to get the task done than to stick to rules and procedures. It's not enough to know that this is happening. A gentle introduction to the reasons behind it and the personal benefits of the approach is needed, particularly for older hands. Spend half an hour thinking through two types of education you need for your staff – understanding of the different world we work in and lifeskills to cope with change.

Feedback In a few areas of business there is actually an increase of dependence on procedures, typically where there is a possibility of legal liability. This can lead to inflexibility and low motivation. There is no clear solution to this dilemma.

Outcome Providing a new perspective has to be handled carefully to avoid demotivating older staff members, but it is essential both for the motivation of younger staff and for the continued good of the company.

Variations None.

Individual	✪✪✪✪
Team	✪✪✪
Group	✪
Fun	✪✪

5.17 | *Energy transfer*

Preparation None.
Running time Two minutes.
Resources None.
Frequency Regular.

Short-term motivation, particularly important in a large group session, is very mood-dependent. However interested you are in a subject, if you are low in energy or depressed you will not be motivated by it. To keep large groups motivated, it is essential you examine your own energy levels first. When you talk to them, will you inspire them or put them to sleep? Content is essential, but so is your delivery. Take two minutes just before you start to liven yourself up. Go outside. Jump up and down. Shout. Punch the air. Do anything that increases your energy level and puts a sparkle into your eyes. Then deliver while you are still on that high.

Feedback It is almost impossible to go over the top with energy. Business guru Tom Peters positively shouts at his audience – and they love it. But beware substituting projected sincerity for energy. This approach, popular among TV evangelists, is rejected by the traditional 'cold' cultures (UK, Scandinavian, Germanic, Eastern seaboard USA), who find it too calculating.

I have known one negative response to energy. A very effective presenter was waking up a Friday evening audience. One of the audience complained that she found the energy of the presenter (who bounces around a lot) too much after a long day. She is the exception. Others might grumble, but still find benefit; most are positive. In the end, the complainer was implying that what she really wanted to do was curl up and go to sleep. Perhaps that was what she should have been doing, but given that she was present, she was certainly in need of energizing.

Outcome Transferring energy to group members is an important motivator – use it, but be aware it is very draining.

Variations See *Warm-ups* (5.44) for other ways of getting energy into a large group. Although transfer of energy is important both for individuals and teams, it should be used sparingly to pull people out of a trough, as it is a short-term motivator.

Individual	✪✪
Team	✪✪
Group	✪✪✪✪
Fun	✪✪✪✪

5.18 | *A little note*

Preparation None.
Running time Five minutes.
Resources Notepad, e-mail or word processor.
Frequency Regular.

This is a trivial-seeming exercise that can deliver an awful lot. When someone has done something well, drop them a thank-you note. It can be anything. Perhaps the person coming to fix your air conditioning took an extra bit of trouble, or a supplier put themselves out to get you a rare item ahead of schedule. It doesn't take much effort (especially with an e-mail address) to run off a note saying thank you. The fact is, though, mostly we don't. So do it. Usually this isn't appropriate for your own staff, as it seems too impersonal, unless for some reason you can't get to see them in the flesh or speak to them by phone.

If the thank you was anything more than trivial, copy in the person's boss. This is beneficial both for the individual, who will be held in better regard by his or her boss, and for the boss.

Feedback   If you are copied in on a thank you note for your staff, or if they show you one, there are two actions to consider. First, add your congratulations. Second, keep a copy on file (if you weren't sent one, ask if you can take one). A fat file of testimonials can be persuasive when your team's future is in question.

Outcome   This is a bit of an unusual one, as the beneficiary may not even work for your company. Even so, it's only by encouraging an environment where thank you is said that you are likely to get similar motivation boosters for your staff.

Variations   Technically a hand-written note has more impact than a word-processed one, which has more impact than an e-mail. While this is true, and I would try to send 'real' letters when a major thank you is required, the huge advantage of e-mail is that it's easy to do. A sent e-mail comes much higher up the appreciation order than a letter you meant to write, but didn't.

Individual	✪✪✪✪
Team	✪✪✪
Group	✪
Fun	✪✪✪

5.19 | *Appropriate appraisal*

Preparation Review past period.
Running time 30 minutes.
Resources Assessment method.
Frequency Occasional.

If you are frustrated by bureaucracy, you may feel that a formal appraisal system is pure paper pushing. You are probably right – yet unless we regularly assess progress against objectives, measure successes and note room for improvement, it is easy to decide that nothing really matters, inducing a demotivating spiral of doubt. Ideally, appraisals should be informal, accurately spotting the moment to check on progress, always catching the staff member doing something right, always discussing ways to improve in a timely way. Sadly, even a manager with the best of intentions is unlikely to deliver on this promise. Reluctantly, we have to turn to a formal system. But make sure that it is used properly. Formal appraisal should be given the highest priority – all too often it is put off because the manager is too busy. Before the appraisal, the manager and staff member should have prepared, pulling together achievements and opportunities for improvement. If the appraisal is driven by a form, don't let the form dictate too much. Be prepared to work round the tick boxes and definitions, as long as the outcome is correct. Oh, and make sure that any outcomes are followed up in the following period.

Feedback Appraisal is extremely important, but can be glossed over because the manager has a lot of them to do, or is uncomfortable talking about performance. This is one of those areas where comfort has to be sidelined. However bad the message, make the items the staff member takes away positive. Not failures, but agreed actions for improvement.

Outcome Most companies recognize the essential nature of assessments, but few give them enough real importance (as opposed to the appearance of importance). By making them truly important, you can have a very positive effect on motivation.

Variations Sometimes you simply don't agree with the assessment system used by your company. See *Faking it* (5.54) for ways to deal with this potentially disastrous situation.

Individual	✪✪✪✪
Team	✪✪
Group	✪
Fun	✪✪

5.20 | **Responsibility**

Preparation None.
Running time Five minutes.
Resources None.
Frequency Occasional.

It seems crazy at first, but you can actually increase motivation by giving someone extra work. Most of us have enough of a craving for power, and being seen to have authority by being given a clear responsibility will act as a motivator. Spend a few minutes thinking through the responsibilities in your gift. They don't have to be major, but rather a good fit to the individual. Could you delegate one or more of those responsibilities to someone who will be motivated by it? Try to hand over responsibility for at least two tasks or areas.

Feedback Responsibility has to be handled with care, as it can be a big source of discomfort. Giving someone extra responsibility when they are already overloaded causes highly demotivating stress. Some very capable people actually dislike responsibility. They are happy continuing to be a highly productive part of the team and don't want responsibility imposed on them. This can be hard to understand for most managers, for whom responsibility tends to be a primary driver.

Unfortunately, just asking someone if they really want the responsibility isn't enough either, because there is often a culture that someone who refuses to take on responsibility is a non-effective team member, who should be downgraded. If you are genuinely offering responsibility as a motivator, make sure there's an escape clause with no penalties attached.

Outcome Giving someone responsibility can offer a wide range of opportunities to expand – from leadership and decision-making to risk-taking and managing your own time. Provided the responsibility is not accompanied by an excessive burden of stress, it's a great motivator.

Variations None.

Individual	✪✪✪✪
Team	✪✪✪
Group	✪
Fun	✪✪

5.21 | *Looking up*

Preparation None.
Running time Five minutes.
Resources A boss.
Frequency Occasional.

When did you last tell your boss he or she was doing a good job? (Let's call him or her Chris to avoid this clumsy 'he or she' business.) When did you last consider rewarding Chris in some way? It seems an unlikely thing to do. After all, it's certainly not your job to motivate your boss. On the other hand, handled correctly it has some very positive benefits. Your boss is human – Chris needs motivation just as much as you, or your staff. From a purely selfish point of view, if you can positively motivate your boss, it can't do your prospects any harm either.

Keep an eye out for things your boss likes. Does Chris have a favourite soft drink or snack? But remember also that motivation doesn't have to be a matter of reward. Just saying 'Thank you' or 'That was brilliant' can work wonders. Or perhaps there's a book that Chris would find really interesting – why not give Chris the chance to borrow it?

Feedback Motivating upwards has to be handled with care to avoid accusations of toadying. Your boss could feel you were trying to win his or her affection, while your peers might consider you a crawler. It is essential to make sure that these motivational acts are occasional and as near as possible spontaneous.

Motivating upwards is a lot easier to do if you are on good social terms with your boss. You don't have to live in each other's lap, but going out for a drink occasionally, chatting about subjects other than work will make it easier. Saying 'That was brilliant' is easy with a complete stranger or someone you get on well with – it's unlikely to work in a very formal relationship.

Outcome Motivating upwards can win you Brownie points with your boss, and is likely to make you more highly regarded. Equally important though, having a motivated boss makes for a better working environment for everyone.

Variations None.

Individual	✪✪✪✪
Team	✪✪
Group	✪
Fun	✪✪

5.22 | *Money, money, money*

Preparation None.
Running time 10 minutes.
Resources None.
Frequency Once.

The purpose of this exercise is to consider how you use money as a motivator. Remember first of all that giving someone extra money generally only has short-term motivational benefits – although not paying enough certainly demotivates in a big way. Think about your staff and the elements of pay. How is the money divided into basic salary and other elements like overtime and performance pay (in different forms)? What do you actually pay people for – what do they have to do to get the money? What influences any extra payments? What influences an increase in salary? Having done this analysis (it may seem obvious, but too many assumptions are made about this sort of detail), think if you got the balance right, or whether there are some items that would be better done differently. The feedback section has some points for stimulus.

Feedback   Are you paying for attendance? Is time all that meaningful, apart from being easy to measure? There's nothing really motivational about payment for time spent 'at work'. Do you have special payment for skills? If so, is there any positive recognition of the use of those skills, or are you really paying for a (potentially worthless) certificate? Do you consider how an individual meets objectives? Does the quality and timeliness of output come into the equation? If not, why not – that's the whole point, isn't it? Do you reward creativity and sensible risk taking? This implies occasional failure, but without it you will have a workforce that never goes beyond the mundane.

Outcome   We take money for granted. This exercise gives you an opportunity to think about how and why we use money to make sure the maximum motivational power is gained from it.

Variations   You may not have direct influence over how money is used in your company – but having thought about it, discuss it with your boss, and encourage him or her to do the same.

Individual	✪✪✪✪
Team	✪✪✪✪
Group	✪
Fun	✪✪

5.23 | **Daggers drawn**

Preparation None.
Running time 10 minutes.
Resources Notepad.
Frequency Once.

This is a preparatory exercise for a situation that you will probably encounter if you lead teams on a regular basis – when individuals or sub-groups build up ill-feeling. If this affects the motivation of the staff you have to intervene. Consider the following three cases and spend a couple of minutes jotting down what you would do in each.

- Paul is getting on Sue's nerves. Sue likes to work head-down, quietly. Paul is always chatting and asking her questions.

- Bill and Tim are IT specialists. Bill, who is an expert in programming languages recommends adopting a new type of language across the company. Tim, who is a business computing expert disagrees, thinks that the recommendation is too theoretical and not based on pragmatic application.

- Mandy is Simon's team leader. Although Mandy is married, she has become increasingly fond of Simon and is beginning to make sexual overtures. Simon is not happy with this situation.

In the first case it may be enough to talk with Paul, but he may be unable to change his behaviour. Look at putting others between them. In the second case do not underestimate the strength of feeling involved. Give the two cooling-off time. Talk to them separately, then bring them together. If sparks still fly you may need to insulate your more technical people from the world, leaving the more pragmatic ones to interface, but at all costs avoid an ivory tower developing. The third case is particularly difficult. It will often be best for all concerned to move either or both of them into different teams.

Feedback Don't agree with my assessments? That's fine. There is no magic answer, nor will the same answer work with everyone. But it is better if you have some practice at thinking through these situations before things happen for real.

Outcome Managing motivation in such circumstances can require radical action, yet without it the entire team can lose their drive.

Variations None.

Individual	✪✪✪✪
Team	✪✪✪✪
Group	✪
Fun	✪

5.24 | ***Fill in the form***

Preparation Process questionnaire.
Running time 10 minutes.
Resources Questionnaire.
Frequency Occasional.

Sometimes it is necessary to use a questionnaire or survey to get a feel for the motivation of a group. It should be drafted carefully to elicit as much as possible the feelings of those involved – and you may need to make it anonymous if you want a genuine response.

Ask both qualitative and quantitative questions (both descriptions and, say, a 1–10 scale), and look for both elements of satisfaction and dissatisfaction with the current position and opportunities to improve things.

Feedback   Using a questionnaire or survey is sometimes absolutely necessary, for example with a large group. However, it should only be regarded as backup information in a normal working environment – if managers don't have a good feel for the motivation of their staff they aren't doing their jobs properly.

A questionnaire or survey should generally be seen as the start of a two-part exercise. It should be combined with feedback to those who have contributed on actual outcomes from their comments. These will only be motivational if something gets done – lots of 'it was very interesting, but not practical' won't improve anything. If the original input was anonymous you will need to disseminate the information widely – and work to remove the lack of trust in your corporate culture that made it necessary to make the input anonymous.

Outcome   It is essential that you have a finger on the pulse of motivation. With anything but a large group, such questionnaires should only be seen as confirming what you already know, but they are still necessary occasionally, as even the best manager will have blind spots.

Variations   Look for different ways of getting this feedback, especially after large group sessions – the conventional questionnaire is getting boring; try to vary the format, means of filling in, etc. Consider prizes for returned forms.

Individual	✪✪✪✪
Team	✪✪✪✪
Group	✪✪✪✪
Fun	✪✪

5.25 | *Time counts*

Preparation None.
Running time One minute.
Resources None.
Frequency Regular.

A classic demotivation technique, which applies across the whole spectrum of individuals, teams and groups, is to prove that you don't value their time.

Take these examples. You ask someone to perform a low priority task immediately, just because you want it done. You call a team meeting and allow it to wander on in an unstructured fashion for the whole afternoon. You invite hundreds of people to a product launch, then leave them standing around in the foyer of the venue clutching a cup of coffee for nearly an hour after the published start time. All common, all illustrating a blatant disregard for other people's time.

So what to do? Don't assume that you have first call on someone's time. For instance, when ringing them, start by asking if they've a couple of minutes to spare. Be aware of other people's priorities. Use good meeting management to avoid time-wasting. And if you end up with a foyer full of people with nothing to do, don't leave them there. If you can, get them into the auditorium and do something (anything) to keep their interest. If it's impossible to go in, organize an event in the foyer – and make sure that you start setting up an hour earlier next time.

Feedback This is a one-minute exercise as it normally involves taking just a minute to step back and see things through someone else's eyes. Sometimes, mainly with large groups, it may be necessary to take drastic action. Part of your preparation for running a group event should be to have a number of contingency activities to keep everyone occupied. The sorts of exercise shown in *Warm-ups* (5.44), and throughout *Instant Teamwork* (see Chapter 6 for more details) make ideal emergency activities.

Outcome If you aren't sympathetic to someone else's values, particularly of something as fundamental as their own time, you are not going to be able to motivate them.

Variations None.

Individual	✪✪✪✪
Team	✪✪✪✪
Group	✪✪✪✪
Fun	✪✪

5.26 | *Portfolio matching*

Preparation None.
Running time 10 minutes.
Resources None.
Frequency Occasional.

Everyone is more likely to be motivated in their job if there is a good match to the portfolio of activities they really want to be doing. Spend a few minutes with someone you want to motivate developing a dream portfolio. Ask them to assume they've won the lottery and never need work for money again. Get them to list the activities they currently do that they'd keep, and which they'd drop. Then add a third column of new activities they would like to start on.

Next, put that list to one side and get them to think about their skills and talents. What are they really good at, or do they feel they might be with appropriate training? Produce a list of skills and use the skills list to act as a filter for the dream portfolio.

Finally, use this refined portfolio to compare with their job. Are there activities that aren't in the portfolio that could be passed on elsewhere? Is there something they aren't doing, but which could be a good match to their portfolio? Don't go for major changes initially – look for some quick hits, but plan to make bigger changes later.

Feedback Getting a better match to what you really want to be doing is a great motivator. Occasionally, this exercise results in someone realizing they want to be working in a different department or a different company. It might seem dangerous in those circumstances, but bear in mind that it's probably better for both of you to have someone leave highly motivated than totally fed up. This technique is a small part of the approach taken in the book *The Chameleon Manager* (see Chapter 6 for more details).

Outcome This is a fun exercise, and if you can make something happen as a result of it, it will be very motivational. Beware, though, of alerting someone to the differences between their portfolio and reality, then doing nothing to help them to bridge the gap.

Variations None.

Individual	✪✪✪✪
Team	✪✪
Group	✪
Fun	✪✪✪✪

5.27 | *The tea bag*

Preparation Collect small items.
Running time One minute.
Resources Small items.
Frequency Regular.

Whether you are motivating a dog or a human being, it's hard to beat the impact of a small, instant reward. Such a reward should be in the 'pocket money' range. When you spot someone doing something really well – a peer or your boss – lay your hands on a reward and get it to them straight away. Speed is of the essence with this technique.

You might find it helpful to stock a drawer with suitable goodies. I have used badges, company give-aways, pens, calculators and more in the past.

Feedback This is one to do by gut feel. Don't feel that you have to schedule rewards ('it's Fred's turn because he hasn't had one yet'). Simply use it to reinforce saying 'That's really good' or 'Thank you.' A good example happened to me a few years ago. The person responsible for allocating accommodation helped me out of a crisis. This was a job that was fraught with confrontation, making the person who did it unpopular. When I was given the news, I dashed to the nearest vending machine, bought a walnut whip and plonked it on the accommodation person's desk. It might be a coincidence, but from that time on, this person (who previously had tended to the bureaucratic) was intensely helpful.

Why 'tea bag'? One of my managers once felt the urge to give me a reward for staying late. He looked around frantically – all he could see was a tea bag, so he gave me that. Despite the fact that I don't drink tea, I was really pleased – demonstrating just how low the value of the reward can be if the sentiment is right.

Outcome A treasure trove of low value goodies is a great way to reinforce the motivational value of a thank you. It costs very little time or money.

Variations None – try it.

Individual	✪✪✪✪
Team	✪✪✪
Group	✪
Fun	✪✪✪✪

5.28 | *Critical response*

Preparation None.
Running time Five minutes.
Resources None.
Frequency Regular.

A useful indicator of motivation is how someone responds to positive criticism. While you have to allow for variations in an individual's feelings about being criticized, in general a well-motivated person will respond well to constructive comments, taking them on-board without feeling threatened. A poorly motivated person, uncertain about their position, will react defensively.

Next time you have a suggestion for improvement to offer to someone whose motivation is of interest to you, watch his or her response carefully. Are they enthusiastic about the opportunity for improvement, or do they seem irritable at the suggestion that things could be better?

Feedback A positive response doesn't have to be one of wholehearted joy. In fact, the recipient of your advice could argue with it and not agree with it, but still be entirely comfortable with your offering advice. Similarly, they might accept your criticism, but in a grudging way that indicates less motivation. You need to be a little flexible in interpretation here.

Make sure that the criticism is valid and stands up on its own – you shouldn't try to test the waters by making a bogus criticism, as this is likely to backfire.

Outcome Sometimes it is quite difficult to detect the level of motivation from simple outward signs. Many people are quite good at hiding feelings in a routine, everyday context. But the provocation of a criticism gives you the opportunity to dig a little beneath the surface and find out what is going on.

Variations Another easy indicator is inclination to help out unasked. Any inclination to a 'more than my job's worth' attitude is a good indicator of poor motivation, just as a tendency to get things done without prompting, to help people out and to go the extra mile reflects good motivation.

Individual	✪✪✪✪
Team	✪✪
Group	✪✪
Fun	✪✪

5.29 | *Confronting troublemakers*

Preparation None.
Running time 10 minutes.
Resources None.
Frequency Occasional.

Every now and then you will come across a motivational troublemaker. This is not someone who goes around smashing things (although such activity doesn't encourage motivation), but someone who constantly undermines morale. They are usually very cynical, suspicious of the company's motives and willing at every opportunity to share their discontent. I have known very good managers who have a blind spot about motivational troublemakers. They see them as a challenge to try to rehabilitate, treading very carefully around the troublemaker's sensitive areas. Unfortunately, during the rehabilitation process (which rarely succeeds) the troublemaker will have been undermining the motivation of everyone within earshot. It's a painful possibility, but like the staff in *The hardest cut* (5.65), it is sometimes necessary to encourage a motivational troublemaker into a different job. Of course, this must be entirely consistent with legal restrictions on constructive dismissal etc. The ideal approach is to find another area where the troublemaker would rather work.

Feedback There's an interesting dilemma when finding the troublemaker a role in a different part of your company. On the one hand, you wouldn't want to drop a disaster on a colleague without warning them. However, you also don't want to put the troublemaker into a new position where he or she may flourish with a label that says 'don't trust me' attached. The ideal is probably to find a job in which the troublemaker would be so motivated that they don't want to upset others, but this can be difficult. Note, by the way, that this exercise is marked very low on fun, but some managers do take a certain enjoyment (or at least satisfaction) from this tactic.

Outcome There's an element of being cruel to be kind here. The fact is, with a real troublemaker, you can make a significant improvement in motivation of a whole group of people by encouraging an individual to take up new interests.

Variations None.

Individual	✪✪✪✪
Team	✪✪✪✪
Group	✪✪✪
Fun	✪

5.30 | *Promises, promises*

Preparation None.
Running time One minute.
Resources Diary.
Frequency Regular.

If ever they bring out a management phrase book, 'Leave it with me' will be translated as 'I'm not going to do anything'. Sadly, a manager's promises often aren't worth the paper they aren't printed on. If you don't fulfil your promises, you are guaranteed to demotivate, whether on a one-off, extreme basis or as a drip-feed of small disappointments.

The first requirement for solving this problem is being aware when you make a promise. Sometimes a casual remark will be interpreted as a promise – if that is likely, consider it to be one. You might mean 'I'll consider it', but if the most likely interpretation is 'I promise to deal with it', you had better do something. Once you are aware of your promises, keep track of them, hence the requirement for a diary. Capture what you have promised, by when. If there is any possibility of not delivering, let the people concerned know as soon as possible and renegotiate. Promise-keeping applies equally to individuals, teams and groups.

Feedback We're all good at making promises, sometimes unconsciously. It might take you a while to spot when you make one. When problems arise because you didn't do something you said you would, work out when and how the promise was made so you can trap similar promises in the future. Note that failing on promises is equally bad for those who work for you, your peers and your boss. Each will find a different way of responding to the reduction of motivation, but you will find them all painful.

Outcome Delivering on promises builds trust and avoids a powerful demotivator. Don't worry if you can't deliver occasionally – provided someone is kept well-informed and is sure that best efforts are being made they will feel that the promise is being fulfilled.

Variations Promise-keeping is closely associated with time management. Consider the wider area through *Instant Time Management* (see Chapter 6 for more details).

Individual	✪✪✪✪
Team	✪✪✪✪
Group	✪✪✪✪
Fun	✪✪

5.31 | *Public praise*

Preparation None.
Running time One minute.
Resources None.
Frequency Regular.

Public praise, used correctly, can be a great motivator. While negative feedback should usually be private, giving recognition in front of others can greatly increase the effect of praise.

This doesn't mean that positive feedback should always be public. Sometimes, particularly with peer feedback, timeliness is more important than visibility. When you have just completed a presentation, it is uplifting to get a thumbs-up sign from a peer whose opinion you value. No one else need be aware of it – it is between the two of you. However, if there's an early opportunity to thank someone in front of others, consider taking it. Make sure that you aren't always praising the same person in public – this can lead to thoughts of favouritism (see *Playing favourites*, 5.64), but use this approach regularly. If the public opportunity is some way off – say a departmental meeting at the end of the month, give more direct and immediate praise to the individual beforehand – don't wait for the big event and leave them feeling that they aren't appreciated for weeks.

Feedback   A fair number of people are shy about public praise. They might blush, or look embarrassed or even tell you that they don't really like it. The vast majority of people who are shy about recognition still get a huge boost from it, they just hate it for those few seconds. Only you can judge if it's a genuine demotivator, but don't be fooled by that embarrassed look.

Outcome   Every performer knows the warm glow that accompanies an enthusiastic round of applause. Compare this with how they'd feel if everyone stared in silence at the end of a performance, then rang up in a week's time to say how much they'd enjoyed it. This is the opportunity that timely public praise presents.

Variations   Public praise works for teams and even for large groups, but the most powerful effect is with individuals.

Individual	✪✪✪✪
Team	✪✪✪
Group	✪✪
Fun	✪✪✪

5.32 | *Change control*

Preparation None.
Running time 15 minutes.
Resources None.
Frequency Occasional.

This is a fundamental motivational consideration, which overlaps with many other techniques. Change is an immensely powerful force, which can motivate or demotivate. It is one of the most common causes of demotivation. When, for example, the banking industry in the UK went through a major change in the 1990s, most branch staff were significantly demotivated. Grouping the branches under a central customer service office cut down on direct customer contact. The pressure to sell insurance turned them into salespeople. But it wasn't what they had joined the bank to do. Three factors caused the demotivation, all of which need to be considered in change. The staff blamed the fresh young managers, because they had no experience of working in a branch. They blamed the move away from customer contact, and they blamed the move to selling, both of which damaged their relationship with customers that might have gone back 20 or 30 years.

If the banks had given more thought to motivation, they would have spotted this coming. Where there is a major change, perform a back-of-an-envelope risk assessment. Will it mean a change in management structure? How will you assure that new managers understand the grass roots business? It can help a lot to give them practical experience at the coalface before expecting them to command. Think particularly about the human impact, from whence most demotivation comes. Bank employees really resented having the relationship with customers taken away from them.

Feedback It's impossible to foresee every risk, but a quick session before embarking on a project can be well rewarded.

Outcome You aren't going to cushion your staff entirely from all change – and some of them will enjoy it. But by reducing the negative impact a lot can be done.

Variations Try to catch the risks before they happen, but if you have to act in retrospect, be generous with accepting fault and being seen to make a difference.

Individual	✪✪✪✪
Team	✪✪
Group	✪
Fun	✪✪

5.33 | *Travel broadens the mind*

Preparation None.
Running time Five minutes.
Resources None.
Frequency Regular.

This is only relevant if your area of work involves visits outside your company, particularly those to other countries or to conferences. Such visits are sometimes referred to as 'jollies', suggesting that they are more for entertainment than real business benefit. In practice, they are usually both. They do have some business value or they wouldn't be undertaken, but they can be a lot of fun, too.

Look at the travel opportunities within your area. See if you can make some of these trips incentives to enhance motivation. Spend a few minutes looking at what is coming up and who would traditionally be sent. Are there other people who could represent the company just as well, but might get more out of it?

Give particular consideration to any travel opportunities you have personally. Could someone else go in your place? Giving away your travel emphasizes the significance of the assignment, adding to its motivational value.

Feedback There is an opportunity for demotivating the people who traditionally went on these trips. However, if you find that a small number of people are hogging the 'jollies', maybe it's time they were shaken up a little.

Bear in mind that not everyone likes to travel. Make sure that you aren't actually irritating someone by sending them. It could be that they hate flying, or it's inconvenient because of something happening in their social life.

Outcome Although such business travel costs the company money, it is money that would have been spent anyway, so this is the ideal subject for motivation, being a very positive incentive without any extra cost to the company. Can't be bad.

Variations Look at other, similar combinations of work and reward. You may attend trade shows or product launches, for instance. These can be quite entertaining, and certainly make a break from office routine.

Individual	✪✪✪✪
Team	✪
Group	✪
Fun	✪✪✪✪

5.34 | *Visible improvement*

Preparation None.
Running time Five minutes.
Resources None.
Frequency Once.

You can only motivate your staff if you are visible. Although this is a self-evident truth, too many managers lock themselves away all day. Spend a few minutes checking through your diary. Are there times blocked off when you will be available in your office? Are there times when you are going to walk among the staff and give them the opportunity to talk about issues – and give them a pat on the back?

Unless you give these activities specific slots in your diary, or make sure you build them around 'natural' breaks, like visiting the coffee machine, meetings will displace them. If your company makes it easy for you to be in an open-plan area with your team, give it a try. Give visibility a chance.

Feedback Management by walking about (MBWA) was very popular in the 1970s and 80s, but has become slightly unfashionable. The existence of other management techniques does not reduce the power of MBWA – and it has the advantage of giving you control of the visibility agenda, rather than leaving it to people to come into your office to see you. However, a total open-door policy makes time management impossible. You have to be able to shut yourself off to deal with personal matters, to think and to be productive. Being visible isn't about being accessible 24 hours a day. For more on practical time management, see the companion volume *Instant Time Management* – details in Chapter 6.

Outcome Visibility says a lot to the staff – that you value them. It also gives you the chance to put the other motivational methods into action.

Variations Find different ways to be visible. Eat in the same place as your team. Try to get in a bit early, so someone who wants to see you can just pop in before the day's work begins. Don't consider this an interruption – it's why you're there.

Individual	✪✪✪✪
Team	✪✪✪✪
Group	✪
Fun	✪✪✪

5.35 | *Smashing the suggestion box*

Preparation None.
Running time 10 minutes.
Resources Notepad.
Frequency Once.

Staff are always coming up with ideas, many of them good. This is highly motivational, provided the ideas are swiftly recognized and acted upon. A good start is to dispose of your company suggestion scheme – or to make sure you don't start one. This seems crazy. I have read books on motivation that encourage you to set up a scheme. But there are two inherent deadly flaws. The first is that most ideas are rejected (after a long wait). Those that are accepted tend to be simplistic cost-saving suggestions (use a plastic widget instead of a metal one), ignoring ideas that are imaginative (base the international meal allowance on a multiple of the price of a Big Mac) or income generating (sell our shoes at nightclubs). The second flaw is that suggestion schemes stress that having ideas isn't part of your job.

Instead, look at ways that ideas can be recognized within the normal management structure. Anyone should be able to e-mail a suggestion to anyone else – and expect a prompt, personal answer. Creativity and idea generating should be part of the recognition system. Any assessment form ought to have a creativity section. Note that many ideas won't work immediately. If an idea looks promising, help the originator to improve it. If there are real problems, feed those back.

Feedback It's all very well making such a radical proposal, but what if you aren't in a position to implement it? First, suggest it (not using the suggestion scheme). Second, make it happen for your staff. Get their ideas through to the right people, and extract the feedback. If your reward system doesn't include creativity assessment, have an unofficial one feeding into your overall ratings. Make use, too, of non-monetary rewards and recognition to highlight good creative performance.

Outcome The whole company will benefit hugely from the extra ideas but, more importantly for motivation, individuals will feel an enormous morale boost when their ideas are taken seriously.

Variations None.

Individual	✪✪✪✪
Team	✪✪
Group	✪
Fun	✪✪✪

5.36 | *E-motivation*

Preparation None.
Running time Five minutes.
Resources E-mail.
Frequency Regular.

Making sure that people get the right message is an essential part of motivation. E-mail may be one of the newest means of communication, but it is intensely valuable to the motivator. E-mail's principle benefit is immediacy. You can have a message in front of someone halfway round the world in minutes. This means if you want to give someone a quick thank you, you can do it almost instantly – and the motivating power of a thank you is greatly enhanced by timeliness.

E-mail is also a very rich means of communication. In all but the most steam-driven e-mail you can include pictures, attach documents and send a very sophisticated message to many people at once, which will help increase the chances of getting your message across and not leaving anyone in demotivating ignorance. Try to make your e-mails personal, though: this always gives them extra impact.

Feedback Beware the negative aspects of e-mail, though. E-mails are so quick to send that you can have one on the way before you've really thought about the content. Read through your e-mails before sending them.

The ease of sending e-mails to many people at once can itself generate a problem. No one likes being flooded with junk mail. Don't copy in people to a document just on the off-chance that it will be useful – but make it very easy for anyone appropriate to receive a copy. One way to avoid this overkill is to make receipt of the messages active rather than passive. Put them onto a bulletin board, or use an e-mail list manager where potential recipients can choose to receive mail (or not) on a subject and can browse through an archive of earlier mail.

Outcome Good use of e-mail is a powerful tool for enhancing communication and hence motivation. Of course you still need good content to go along with the enhancements.

Variations Consider different ways to enhance communications. See *Publish and be damned* (5.4).

Individual	✪✪✪✪
Team	✪✪✪
Group	✪✪
Fun	✪✪

5.37 | *Ask them*

Preparation Opportunity to chat.
Running time 10 minutes.
Resources None.
Frequency Once.

We are sometimes too devious for our own good, devising cunning tests to assess motivation, but never asking people what works for them. This technique is simple in theory, harder to do.

Fit the subject into a general developmental meeting or informal chat, as it will feel artificial if you arrange a meeting specifically for the purpose. Ask your subject what motivates him or her and (as a separate question) what demotivates. Get an immediate reaction, then probe that response. The response may be a knee-jerk element like money. Take this on board, but look beyond it. Stress that you aren't looking for a specific answer – you genuinely want to know what will help them to get on. If they struggle, talk through motivational roles (see page 11) and motivating factors. A valuable question to cover is 'What could I do better?' The fact that you value their opinion enough to ask this (provided you pay some attention to the answer) can be highly motivating.

Feedback   Although it seems most natural to apply this technique to your staff, it is equally useful for your peers and your bosses. In such circumstances, you may approach the subject by talking about the motivation of someone else, then turn it round to them. Even if you have a bad memory, don't take notes; it looks manipulative. Note-taking should be done alone, as soon as possible after the event.

Outcome   This won't produce a definitive set of drivers. Few people are honest enough (even with themselves) to open up entirely. There may be some suspicion of your motives, and you will probably get an unnatural stress on demotivating tranquilizers (pay, conditions, etc). Even so, bearing in mind that motivation is very individual, this is a valuable exercise.

Variations   This exercise can be undertaken with a team, but emphasize that you want to look at those factors that influence the team *as a team*, not as individuals.

Individual	✪✪✪✪
Team	✪✪✪
Group	✪
Fun	✪✪

5.38 | *Lasers and dry ice*

Preparation Prepare and rehearse.
Running time Five minutes.
Resources Varied.
Frequency Occasional.

Short-term motivation is highly dependent on mood. A powerful combination of imagery and music can dramatically influence feelings. If you are planning a major event, making use of multimedia, technology, dramatic music and practically anything that is an assault on the senses is a valid option to manipulate mood and hence motivation.

You won't do this in five minutes. In fact, since it must be highly professional to be effective, you are unlikely to implement it yourself at all. What is useful at the planning stage, though, is to spend five minutes thinking about the shape of the event – where you want to inject a dose of motivation, and the style of multimedia blitz which will best suit your attendees.

Feedback Glitz without any underlying content has a very short shelf life – it will swiftly switch from motivation to demotivation once it appears that there is nothing behind the smoke and mirrors. There has to be appropriate content, too.

If you are concerned about manipulation – don't be. There is no secret about what you are doing, and most people will get a lot of enjoyment out of it. This assumes, though, that it is done well, hence the need for a professional team providing the multimedia, rehearsal to spot any glitches, and plenty of preparation. Beware at all costs of half-hearted glitz. If you can't afford to do it properly, don't do it at all.

Outcome This sort of cheerleading motivation won't have a long-term impact, but it is very valuable as a foundation on which to build content-driven motivation. Without the foundation, the best content can still slip away.

Variations You aren't going to have a sound-and-light show with fireworks as part of a one-to-one discussion. However, it's worth remembering the impact of multimedia when communicating to individuals and teams. Do your e-mails have to be always plain text? Do your team meetings have to be always supported just by a paper agenda and a whiteboard?

Individual	✪✪
Team	✪✪
Group	✪✪✪✪
Fun	✪✪✪✪

5.39 | *Break time*

Preparation Schedule breaks.
Running time Five minutes.
Resources None.
Frequency Regular.

In group sessions, careful management of breaks is essential. Regular breaks will restore drooping attention, remove distractions (like the need to go the toilet) and improve motivation to get on with the agenda. Such breaks should be scheduled but, if possible, be prepared to modify them in response to the mood of the group. This is easy with a small seminar, but less practical with a group of 400 people, where you will need on the whole to stick to a schedule.

A common mistake with breaks is to make them too infrequent and too long. It's much better to have chunks of effort lasting 40 minutes to an hour with five-minute breaks than a whole morning concentrating and then a long gap. Be particularly careful with the lunch break. This is very dependent on the location and the group. It should not be too long, as people can become bored or drift back to work (if appropriately located), never returning to the session. However, people will need time to eat and to have a few minutes away from it all. A good rule of thumb is to allow enough time to get everyone through the feeding process, plus 15 minutes spare time.

Feedback Sometimes breaks will be resented. Everything is going so well that people don't want to stop. They want to get on with it. Persevere with the breaks nonetheless. However much they feel that they are progressing, short breaks will help things to go better and to keep on going well. They improve creativity and stop the group getting into a rut. Keep the breaks.

Outcome Without breaks, individuals get stale, group morale tails off and the outcome is rapidly diminishing motivation. Whatever the pressure to keep going, make sure breaks occur.

Variations Taking breaks is just as important for individuals and teams, although here it is often seen more as time management – see Chapter 6 for more information.

Individual	✪✪✪
Team	✪✪✪
Group	✪✪✪✪
Fun	✪✪✪

5.40 | *Firm but fair*

Preparation Plan the agenda and establish available recourses of action.
Running time Five minutes.
Resources None.
Frequency Occasional.

Motivation is usually about positive actions. Even when things go wrong, the motivational approach is not to criticize, but to help those involved to learn and improve for the future. However, it's a mistake to confuse being positive with being soft. Now and again someone actively refuses to learn and continues producing the same, avoidable failures. In such circumstances, it is motivational to be strict with the person involved. Not necessarily for that person, but certainly for everyone else, who will feel put-upon, resenting your softness. The message will become diffuse and confusing.

In such circumstances don't haul the individual over the coals in public – the result is a negative atmosphere, even for those who really disliked the individual or what they were doing. Instead take them aside. Make your views on what has been happening and how you want things to change explicit. Set out a clear agenda for improvement. And make sure that they stick to it. Explain in detail what will happen if they don't.

Feedback Occasionally, even after making the situation crystal clear, you will find an individual who continues not to learn. Here again you will need to be firm. Carry through the threatened action – never make a threat you aren't prepared to carry out. Exactly what it was will depend on the disciplinary procedures of your company, but for the benefit of everyone you should endeavour to help this individual to find different employment – whether working for you, another part of your company or another company – in which they will be able to act more effectively. Keeping a member of staff in an inappropriate role helps no one.

Outcome Even the person who has repeatedly failed is likely to have an improvement in motivation when your actions result in greater success for them. But the big payback here is in the motivation of the rest of your team, who see that they are no longer carrying this individual.

Variations None.

Individual	✪✪✪
Team	✪✪✪✪
Group	✪
Fun	✪

5.41 | *Celebration time*

Preparation Choose venue.
Running time An evening.
Resources Cost of celebration.
Frequency Occasional.

Every now and then there is a need to celebrate. We need rites of passage to mark major events. Perhaps your team has delivered 150 per cent effort to get a project completed on time. Perhaps they have got you a promotion through superb effort. Such events should not happen often – twice a year at most – and they should not become routine or they lose impact.

With a small group, the best approach is probably a celebration dinner. It may seem trite, but it works (as long as the company pays). It is a win–win for motivation, because the team gets the message the company has noticed their efforts, and they also grow closer through social interaction. With larger gatherings, all the way up to a whole department or company, you will need to be more imaginative, but the concept is the same.

Feedback Beware the annual sales awards syndrome. Motivational celebrations should be one-offs. Anything predictable and expected every year loses motivational value. Try to make team celebrations exclusive. The whole focus is on the team. The team leader should be there – because they are part of the team – but not a more senior manager or director, even if he or she is paying. Exclude spouses and partners, too. Like it or not, they will dilute the feeling of 'we did this together'.

Outcome As well as the benefits already described, such celebrations act as a wake. Although it is impossible to keep up indefinitely the high-pressure drive that is needed for the sort of success that is being celebrated, the pressure will be missed when it is over. The event helps the team to say 'That's over, now we're doing something different' – and gives an opportunity to review and fix in the memory the highlights and disasters of the shared experience.

Variations Don't miss this opportunity if the company is too tight to pay – if necessary the managers should pay for it themselves.

Individual	✪✪✪
Team	✪✪✪✪
Group	✪✪✪✪
Fun	✪✪✪✪

5.42 | *Train tracks*

Preparation Check assessments and past training.
Running time 10 minutes.
Resources Individual meeting.
Frequency Occasional.

Gross generalization: training motivates. Like all generalizations this is not entirely true, as the wrong sort of training is a turn-off. See *Objective view* (5.66) for an example of how training with unclear objectives can demotivate. However, provided the staff member feels that the training is worthwhile, being sent on training courses has a positive effect.

The reason is not difficult to understand. Sending someone on a course, instead of having them occupied in productive work, generates a stronger message than words can convey. It says that we value you as an individual, we see that you have a future with this company and are worth investing in. Not only that, it says that we think you can go further, and we are going to put money into getting you there. Next time you think about training, consider the benefits as well as the costs.

Feedback Least effective motivationally are large-scale events that everyone attends. They can provide a lot of motivation on the day, but don't give any message of being especially valued. Next comes technical training. This makes the individual feel valued, but be wary of suggesting that they are incompetent. Also avoid using such courses with 'naturals' who can (say) pick up word processing in five minutes and will be intensely bored one hour into a course. Most valuable for motivation is development training, improving interpersonal, creative or management skills. This really says 'You are going places, and we want to help you to grow'.

Outcome Focused training is a superb winner, both for motivating and increasing skills. Don't waste your training budget on too much mundane technical training if you can get that on the job; look for development instead.

Variations Although not as powerful as training, giving individuals developmental books is also motivational (and much cheaper). It's amazing how companies are willing to spend thousands on courses, but rarely spend £10 to £20 on a book.

Individual	✪✪✪✪
Team	✪✪✪
Group	✪
Fun	✪✪✪

5.43 | *Peerless peers*

Preparation None.
Running time Five minutes.
Resources None.
Frequency Occasional.

Most of us concentrate on our staff when motivating. Sometimes we think about giving the boss a morale boost (see *Looking up*, 5.21). But few of us consider our peers. In fact, there's a considerable opportunity here. In every walk of life, people find it helpful to talk to and learn from others who are going through similar experiences – your peers are a natural in-company support group.

There's also a lot that can be done with a few words. Where you wouldn't expect to reward your peers directly, a pat on the back and a compliment on something they've just done can work wonders. After all, as they say at the Academy Awards, there's nothing more important than recognition by your peers.

When thinking about motivating peers, remember mutuality, too. It's not just about being able to help others; they can help you, too. After all, even you need motivation occasionally.

Feedback One of the reasons we sometimes don't motivate our peers is out of jealousy or competitive concern. After all, you hardly want to give them a hand up so they can trample all over you. This isn't necessarily a very logical position, though. If they do get in a position of power over you, it wouldn't be a bad thing to have helped them on their way. And helping someone else to get on doesn't have to be detrimental to your career.

Don't take the 'support group' example too literally. Some see support groups as weak people who can't manage without help. This is something quite different – it's the sort of professional networking that all hot business people crave.

Outcome Except for close friends you might find it strange to be motivating your peers, but persevere.

Variations This may be a team activity if you are in a peer-based team, but for managers, your staff form your real team, and your peers form a more diffuse group.

Individual	✪✪✪✪
Team	✪✪✪
Group	✪
Fun	✪✪

5.44 | *Warm-ups*

Preparation None.
Running time Five minutes.
Resources None.
Frequency Occasional.

A warm-up technique can be invaluable in getting a team or a large group motivated. There's a whole book of them in *Instant Teamwork* (see Chapter 6) from which this one is adapted.

Get the entire group standing up. If you are performing this exercise as a delaying tactic (eg to keep motivation up while an auditorium is prepared), explain that there has been a delay, so you are going to warm them up first. Ask them to get together in teams whose surnames start with the same letter (with a smaller group, make this surnames A to C etc as appropriate – you will need to prepare this ahead of time). If they haven't achieved this after two minutes, stop them anyway. Now get them teamed up with people who drive the same make of car. After a minute or so, stop them again. Finally, ask them to join people with the same colour of underwear.

Feedback Allow more time for the first session, because it becomes easier with practice. Initially there will be some tentative asking around, until someone takes the initiative and stands on a table, shouting their selection at the top of their voice. An excellent aspect of this exercise is that the bigger the numbers are, the better. I have used it with several hundred people to great effect.

Outcome Waiting for an event to begin can be demotivating – using a warm-up relieves this problem. It also has a positive motivational effect of sending a group into action with a more constructive and energized frame of mind.

Variations You can use almost anything to group people, although ideally it should have relatively few options (age, for instance, is too broad). Colour of underwear is a great finisher, because it has a slight frisson of naughtiness, leaving the participants on an energetic high. Don't be tempted to replace it with something tamer, whatever the audience.

Individual	✪
Team	✪✪✪✪
Group	✪✪✪✪
Fun	✪✪✪✪

5.45 | *Personal projects*

Preparation None.
Running time Five minutes.
Resources None.
Frequency Occasional.

Often the opportunity to undertake a personal project is a great motivator. However much someone is a team player, there is something special about a solo achievement. Consider giving your staff the opportunity to undertake a personal project. This should be something that can be undertaken in a relatively short time – either a regular couple of hours a week, or the whole project in a concentrated day. It should have potential benefit to the company, but part of the attraction of such a project is that it could have a much higher risk of failure than a conventional exercise.

Have a five-minute session with your staff, describing the concept. You might have a specific project in mind, or want them to come up with something. There might not be a burning issue right now – make it clear that there is no stigma attached to putting the personal project slot on a back-burner until an idea or requirement comes up.

How much structure you then give to the project depends on the individual. Your involvement could be limited to 'Give me some feedback when you've achieved something' or a weekly five-minute update on progress.

Feedback Don't fall into the trap of considering this time wasting. Make sure that it's a small enough proportion of time that it won't have any real effect on the individual's ordinary work. Many personal projects may be failures, but some will deliver spectacularly. Be prepared to support and further a positive outcome.

Outcome There are people who really don't want to do this sort of thing. But for many, the opportunity to work on something that's really theirs is a superb motivator. It's the sort of thing they put effort into in their own time, because it gives them a buzz. As with all good motivators, it's a win–win.

Variations This approach could also be applied at a team level, but there's less special impact then.

Individual	✪✪✪✪
Team	✪✪
Group	✪
Fun	✪✪✪

5.46 | *No comment*

Preparation None.
Running time Five minutes.
Resources None.
Frequency Once.

Next time you ask someone for an opinion in an area where you have your own strong views, or the company has a strong line, try to detach yourself from the process. There is a very strong tendency to come in with your own opinion or the official line as soon as it becomes obvious that the thoughts you are hearing differ from it.

This time, hold back your opinion. Don't comment on what is being said. Offer encouragement to whoever is speaking to give a full view, but don't criticize or give any direction. Only respond when they have fully got their message across. Make sure that what you say is a response and not a speech – don't trot out the party line like a politician who gives the answer he intends to give whatever the question is, respond to what has been said as honestly as possible.

If you agree, strongly reinforce their point – and say what you'll do about it. If you disagree, explain why.

Feedback It's normally very tempting to jump in to 'correct' someone as soon as they say something that doesn't fit your views. Even if you don't jump in at the start, the natural tendency is to spend much of the time developing your counter-argument, rather than truly listening. Yet listening is essential if you are to convey worth to the speaker. If you practise this holding back technique enough, you may even get to the stage where other people demand your view, because they feel that you are being left out.

Outcome Listening and being seen to listen, then acting on what you have heard, gives a strong message that you value what you are hearing, and by implication that you value the speaker. The motivational power is considerable.

Variations None.

Individual	✪✪✪✪
Team	✪✪
Group	✪
Fun	✪✪

5.47 | *Own pocket*

Preparation Buy something.
Running time Five minutes.
Resources Small amount of cash.
Frequency Occasional.

This technique can be used in association with *The tea bag* (5.27) or *Toys for boys* (5.57), but it stands alone as either technique can be used with or without this approach. Both these techniques (and *Gift aid*, 5.11), emphasize the value of gifts over cash. You can, in some circumstances, emphasize this motivational value by buying the gift from your own pocket, rather than on company expenses.

Obviously, you don't want to put yourself hugely out of pocket, but it's arguable that the good manager (or presenter) will be prepared to suffer a small outgoing to gain the return.

You will have to be a little subtle about this. Loudly announcing that you are out of pocket in the process isn't going to make anyone motivated. It should either be simply the sort of gift that you are very unlikely to buy on expenses (for instance, a chocolate bar) or phrased in such a way that it seems likely that you bought it.

Feedback This is a technique to be used with some care. The gift should be of low value, and you should make sure that it is given in such a way that it is clearly a thank you for something done in the work context, so there is no danger of it being taken as a sexual overture. It is also an approach that will devalue with overuse. Just as swearing has more impact if used infrequently, this sort of gift is particularly special if kept sparingly. Even with birthdays or Christmas, it is probably more effective to be an occasional giver, as it is then seen as something special. (This is with respect to work contacts; your family may expect more regularity!) As always (see *Playing favourites*, 5.64), be careful to avoid the appearance of favouritism.

Outcome A purchase from your own pocket speaks significantly more strongly than anything an expense account can do.

Variations None.

Individual	✪✪✪✪
Team	✪✪✪
Group	✪✪
Fun	✪✪✪

5.48 | *Empty desk syndrome*

Preparation None.
Running time Five minutes.
Resources None.
Frequency Once.

This is an unlearning exercise. I have seen books that suggest checking on motivation levels by looking at staff and their surroundings. If they have a neat tidy desk, with very little on it and they are dressed smartly, they are well-motivated. If there is chaos on the desk or dress is untidy, they are badly motivated.

If you have been exposed to this sort of material, or have an underlying sense that it is true, fight it. People work better, and are best motivated, in a comfortable environment. Some like tidiness, some like organized chaos (it might look a mess, but chances are they can find the essentials very quickly). A similar observation applies to dress codes. When I was a senior manager in a large company, I was entirely comfortable with wearing suits. However, since running my own company, I find that I am significantly more comfortable without the suit. I still wear it when required, but don't find it motivational.

If there is any truth in tidiness, it is that neat, tidy desks imply the team has limited motivation to the task. Every ultra-high performing team I have had the privilege to be part of has operated in a degree of mess, because the team focus is so strong that the environment disappears. Empty pizza boxes and piled up reports may upset the tidy small mind, but they can also reflect ultra-high motivation.

Feedback When you accept an indicator like 'a tidy desk' or 'dresses smartly' you are falling back, perhaps unconsciously, into considering a person as an interchangeable component. See page 9 for more on the dangers of this dated fallacy.

Outcome The message of this exercise is simple, but widely ignored. You can't depend on 'standard' indicators to determine the motivation of your staff – you have to *know* them.

Variations Be wary of other standardized indicators of this type.

Individual	✪✪✪✪
Team	✪✪✪
Group	✪
Fun	✪✪

5.49 | *Change as motivator*

Preparation Background information.
Running time 30 minutes.
Resources Team meeting.
Frequency Occasional.

Change is often a demotivating factor. We all find comfort in 'the way things have always been' and tradition. Change undermines the status quo and makes us feel uncomfortable. Yet without change there is inertia and boredom – and like it or not, change is here to stay and ever-accelerating.

It is possible to use change as a positive agent for motivation. Often the gut reaction of staff to change is to try to counter it. To say how it has been tried before, or it will never work, or they didn't join the company to do this sort of thing. Turn the situation round. Explain the need for change, then consult them as experts in what to change and how to make it work. Don't make the possibility of it not working an option – look for ways to make things succeed.

Feedback   Initially you will get the knee-jerk responses, asserting that the change won't work. Some people will never come round to change, but by squashing any negatives at this stage you will have a good chance of carrying most of the staff with you. Next, you will probably be given the solution of throwing a lot of cash/people/resources at the problem. As new governments soon discover, this is rarely an acceptable long-term measure. Point out the implications of huge spending and help the staff to move towards solutions that fit within the financial (and other) constraints you may have. Now you should begin to get some effective suggestions. Even if you don't, the simple process of being consulted and taken seriously will help motivation.

Outcome   This approach turns change into a motivational factor, a rather handy development given the certainty of change in the business environment.

Variations   Try this approach of turning the factor on its head and getting staff to make it work with other demotivators.

Individual	✪✪✪✪
Team	✪✪✪✪
Group	✪
Fun	✪✪

5.50 | *The genuine article*

Preparation Produce scenarios.
Running time 10 minutes.
Resources Sounding board.
Frequency Twice.

Communication is a key factor in motivation. How well you communicate will often determine how well you can motivate. The most powerful means of communication for these purposes is direct, face to face. Unfortunately, it is difficult to judge how good you are at this.

Produce a few short scenarios of motivational communication. Try one where you congratulate someone on an excellent piece of work, one where you go through a mistake someone has made, one where you discuss life goals (what someone really wants to do) and one where you welcome a group of people to a company event. Find a sounding board – someone to listen and note how you come across. They should check how genuine you seem, your body language (don't fold your arms, for example), your eye contact, your tone of voice (watch out for dropping your tone at the end of a sentence) and the way you speak – anything that can alter motivation.

After the session get some feedback. Look for areas to improve. Put together an action plan – and book your sounding board for a review.

Feedback There's an old (not very good) joke along the lines of 'When you can fake being genuine you've got it made'. What you say is important, but the way you say it will have an equal impact. It's not enough to be genuine, you've got to put it across. Many of us, for instance, find it difficult to praise and resort to a joking delivery and reduced eye contact. Praise that sounds as if you don't mean it is totally wasted.

Outcome Getting honest but constructive feedback on how you come across is very valuable. Without it, it's almost impossible to be sure what your messages really say.

Variations Try videoing this exercise. Almost everyone cringes at the sight of themselves on video – go beyond the personal embarrassment to the specifics of your performance.

Individual	✪✪✪✪
Team	✪✪✪✪
Group	✪✪✪✪
Fun	✪✪

5.51 | *The rumour mill*

Preparation None.
Running time 10 minutes.
Resources Team meeting.
Frequency Once.

There are few things with the same power to crush motivation as a rumour. The frightening thing about rumours is that they seem airy and insubstantial, but they can create wholesale damage. They're very easy to start, and much harder to stop.

Hold a 10-minute rumour dumping session with your team. Find out as much as possible about the sort of rumours that are common. If they're about the company – its future, what it is doing – look at ways that you can get company information spread more effectively. Could you use an intranet or other computer systems? Is there any reason why employees shouldn't have free access to most company information? If the rumours are about individuals, it might be worth talking with those individuals or their managers to take action to change things. Your aim should be to kill rumours by spreading more accurate, if less salacious, information.

Feedback Favourite topics for rumours are redundancies, relocations, staff leaving the company, salaries and emotional entanglements. You won't be able to eradicate every rumour, but it should be possible to minimize the threat of demoralizing business-oriented rumour by ensuring that your staff have appropriate information.

Outcome The truth might not be particularly pleasant, but it's almost always better than drawn-out uncertainty. In the case of a lot of rumours, it's also a lot better than the rumour. There's a big motivational opportunity here as long as you are prepared to be more open about company information.

Variations This is labelled a one-off exercise, but it would be useful to repeat it occasionally and to try it with different groups of people to see what the state of the rumour mill is. Note that the quick exercise is identifying rumours – putting in place the appropriate information flows may be anything but instant.

Individual	✪✪✪✪
Team	✪✪✪✪
Group	✪
Fun	✪✪

5.52 | *Absolute sports*

Preparation None.
Running time 10 minutes.
Resources Team meeting.
Frequency Once.

There is no doubt of the motivation that can come from sport, and many people find sporting activities more motivational than work. While this is more a criticism of their work than an affirmation of sport, it would be foolish to overlook sport's potential.

Explore the different sporting interests of the team. Is there a common interest that they can undertake? Is there something no one has done that they would all like to try out? It can be anything from ice-skating to water polo.

This exercise has to be undertaken with care. Participation must be voluntary, with no stigma attached from not taking part. Ideally, you should only go ahead if everyone wants to, otherwise there will soon be a clique. Care should be taken about timing (eg not using Sundays if there are Christians in the team), and some thought should be given to ensure that the sport won't be divisive if some members of the team are much better than others.

Feedback Some companies actively look for sports-playing individuals when recruiting on the theory that they will be better team members. This is spurious. An enthusiastic tennis player, for example, will be less of a team player than a member of a choir or a history society. It is more a left-over of the public school/military emphasis on sport than a valid observation. Arguably, enthusiastic sports players lack creative drive, because their chosen activity doesn't produce anything – perhaps they should be actively avoided.

Outcome There are two potential benefits. With an individual activity, like ice-skating, there is an opportunity to build support within the team, as less able members are helped out by more able (make sure they don't get fed up with this role, though). A team activity has obvious opportunity for increased bonding and internal motivation.

Variations Look at other, non-sporting team activities. Anything from a pub quiz to a visit to a theme park or putting on a team pantomime can be effective (provided the team leader joins in).

Individual	✪✪
Team	✪✪✪✪
Group	✪
Fun	✪✪✪

5.53 | *Quality content*

Preparation Plan.
Running time 10 minutes.
Resources None.
Frequency Regular.

When you are planning a group session, put a few minutes aside to consider quality of content. Try to assess what you would really get out of the session as an attendee. What would others get out of it (for example, your employer)? Which bits would you get all excited about – and which would you fall asleep in?

If all else fails, you can insert mood-lifting exercises (see *Lasers and dry ice*, 5.38 or *Warm-ups*, 5.44). In fact, these are valuable anyway. But they should not be crutches to support a session that lacks content or is boring. Take the worst points of your event and find a way to improve them – not by a few per cent, but an order of magnitude. Nothing has to be boring – find a way to make it exciting. If the problem is a total lack of content, drop that session. Sometimes, you will find the entire event lacks content. Either cancel it or start from scratch – otherwise you will end up with seriously demotivated attendees.

This exercise may result in radical surgery. Don't let that put you off – sometimes tuning has to be anything but fine.

Feedback   It's easy to rebel. Of course your session has content, that's the whole point, isn't it? The trouble is, we often engage in large-group activities because we ought to. We might decide, for instance, that we need a company-wide session because customer service is poor. This may be true, but it doesn't say anything about the content you devise, and it's tempting to fill it with froth. Don't assume that a worthy cause implies effective content.

Outcome   It is essential to take a step back like this, because big events rapidly gain a momentum of their own and good intentions can overlook poor delivery. Not only can lack of content directly reduce motivation, it also irritates people to see a lot of money being spent on a worthless event.

Variations   None.

Individual	✪✪
Team	✪
Group	✪✪✪✪
Fun	✪✪

5.54 | *Faking it*

Preparation None.
Running time Five minutes.
Resources Assessment method.
Frequency Once.

Another activity (*Appropriate appraisal* 5.19) looks at the motivational value of performance assessments. However, there is a problem if managers don't agree with the company's appraisal system. The temptation is to confide in the staff member. A classic example I have come across is a system giving each staff member a rating, which is forced to lie on a normal distribution. Along with other managers, I was required to tell individuals that they had been rated lower than I wanted them to be, because the system demanded it.

The temptation to blame the system is huge. You can side with the staff member against 'them'. Unless you are a sadist this will be very reassuring for you. Yet it can result in the staff member going away with the wrong message. Fight the inclination. Your actual response should depend on the likely outcome of the appraisal.

If the system forces you to give them a rating (or equivalent) that is lower than you would like, but the outcome is still generous, concentrate on the outcome. If there is a mechanism for tweaking the outcome to compensate for special performance, use it. In the worst circumstance of an unjustified poor result with no mitigating circumstances, explain the mechanism that produced it with no value judgements. Discuss with the person how you can make sure things are different next time – fix his or her vision on the future, not the past.

Feedback The particular problem you have with your system may not be the same (although they usually relate to a mechanical component), but the response will be. Note that, while you shouldn't blame the system, you should do everything you can behind the scenes to fight an inappropriate mechanism.

Outcome This is a damage-limitation exercise. You might find it personally quite painful not to blame the system, but you need to take that flak – being responsible for other people isn't always fun.

Variations None.

Individual	✪✪✪✪
Team	✪✪
Group	✪
Fun	✪

5.55 | *Spice it up*

Preparation None.
Running time Five minutes.
Resources None.
Frequency Regular.

Variety is the spice of life – and is essential for motivation. When dealing with individuals, undertake *Portfolio matching* (5.26) first. Looking at what the individual does now and what his or her personal portfolio indicates, put together an action plan for enrichment. Look at ways of increasing the individual's skills; look at areas of high personal interest and for opportunities for an individual to be responsible for a whole task. Ensure the individual's day and week is broken up to give variety.

Divide a large group event into several activities during the day – typically no more than one hour per session. If the whole event is focused on a single topic, break up that topic and come at it from different ways. However the session breaks down, use time-outs – 5- or 10-minute episodes of doing something completely different to keep the group fresh (see *Instant Teamwork* in Chapter 6 for more details). Once you have outlined the session, take a couple of minutes to assess it for variety.

Feedback Sometimes variety can be a change of pace or environment. If you can't motivate by changing topic, move the people to different locations. Enrichment is a natural step as we move from the 20th century, input-oriented view of organization charts, job slots and evaluation to the 21st century, output-oriented view of people-centred work and flexible response. Some will find it difficult, as it means individuals taking more personal responsibility. The unions and old-fashioned managers may fight it too, as it represents a reduction in their power base. But the move is unstoppable; the question is whether you will cope, not whether it will happen.

Outcome Job enrichment increases motivation, gives better retention of key staff and better productivity. It's sometimes difficult to see the need for variety, especially under pressure. Like breaks (see *Break time* 5.39), variety can seem a waste of precious time. But without variety productivity plummets, originality withers and accuracy falls.

Variations None.

Individual	✪✪✪
Team	✪✪✪
Group	✪✪✪✪
Fun	✪✪✪

5.56 | *Team supporters*

Preparation None.
Running time 15 minutes.
Resources None.
Frequency Once.

Providing people with support in what they are doing underpins almost all motivation, and a lack of support is demotivating in its own right. Some companies draw their organization charts upside down to emphasize that the manager supports the staff, rather than the other way round. Apart from setting direction and keeping on course, a key role of management is supporting the people who get things done.

Sometimes this is about concrete matters, like having the tools to get the job done (see *Tooling up*, 5.9). But often it is a matter of being there – of being seen as someone who will provide support, rather than simply giving orders or sitting in meetings. The immediate exercise you should undertake is looking at how you can put this across to your staff, making them aware that it is part of your role. It should be clear that this doesn't make you a dogsbody, but forms an important part of what you do.

Feedback A useful secondary exercise is to think about just who comes to you for support, and in what circumstances. Are there specific people who do and don't? Are there certain areas that are no-go? Are you consciously or unconsciously refusing support in these areas? Is it nothing to do with you anyway? To perform this task properly you need to have a good picture of your own role and what you want to do. Consider doing an exercise like *Portfolio matching* (5.26) on yourself to make this clearer.

Outcome Support can be directly motivational, but it is also an essential foundation for many of the other techniques in this book.

Variations Providing support expands naturally from the individual to the team. It is a slightly different prospect with a large group – the group will need support mainly in formal terms (having a clear agenda, housekeeping details), but individuals often need support in a strange environment like this, which must be catered for.

Individual	✪✪✪✪
Team	✪✪✪
Group	✪✪✪
Fun	✪✪

5.57 | *Toys for boys*

Preparation None.
Running time Five minutes.
Resources Giveaways.
Frequency Occasional.

Actually toys for anyone. People like getting surprise gifts. Consider having spot prizes in meetings – this works particularly well with large groups. A good way to do this is to make the prize the result of answering a question that no one can sensibly know the answer to. This is quite different from the *Tea bag* (5.27). There the gift is a specific, speedy response to an action. Its purpose is to say 'Thank you' and 'Well done'. Similarly, it is different from *Gift aid* (5.11) where an appropriate (and probably quite valuable) gift is used as a more personal alternative to a cash bonus. This technique is about lifting morale by using the sense of excitement and fun that awarding a prize or surprise gift gives.

Amass a collection of attractive small goodies – they can be anything from a novelty item like a balloon or a badge, through to practical but attractive gifts like books or software, to a high-tech gadget.

Feedback Some care has to be taken in the use of giveaways. It's best if the reason for getting it does not involve skill, as this can be divisive and actually reduces motivation in those who don't win. It's also important not to get expectations up too high. I was once at a conference where they announced a spot prize and a car burst through the screen. Everyone was thrilled – they were giving away a car! When it turned out they were actually letting the winner have free use of it for a year – still a very attractive prize – everyone was disappointed. The mishandled expectations undid any positive motivational effects.

Outcome An excellent building block in a group's motivational structure.

Variations None.

Individual	✪✪✪
Team	✪✪✪
Group	✪✪✪✪
Fun	✪✪✪✪

5.58 | *Two-faced management*

Preparation None.
Running time Five minutes.
Resources Notepad.
Frequency Once.

This is a one-off exercise, but you are likely to have to undertake the real thing a number of times. Imagine that there was a new policy in your company that you didn't agree with. Come up with a specific example for the exercise (there may be something already under way in your company). First spend a couple of minutes planning your upward-pointing campaign. What could you do to encourage your bosses not to go ahead with this action?

Then take a couple of minutes on your local campaign. Assume that the policy has gone through despite your best efforts. How will you sell it to your staff, despite your opposition? Is there anything you can do to shield them from its excesses? Make sure that you don't sell it by distancing yourself from the company – setting up an 'us and them' position is only a short-term motivational tactic. Long-term it demotivates. Your staff might find it easy to identify with you when you blame 'them' but they won't respect you for it.

Feedback   This is a difficult one for honest managers. After all, it seems to require you to be two-faced. This is particularly difficult when you consider how important it is to be genuine with your staff if you are to motivate them. The paradox is that in both stages you are doing your best for your staff's motivation, in the first place by trying to stop the unfortunate development occurring and then by helping them to accept the inevitable. It might seem also that it will damage your status with your superiors, but it may actually have a positive effect.

Outcome   Gaining practice at this sort of balancing act is essential, especially for new leaders and managers. Note particularly the requirement not to blame 'them'.

Variations   A special case of the two-faced manager is *Faking it* (5.54), which looks at handling appraisals, where the manager is not happy with the appraisal mechanism.

Individual	✪✪✪✪
Team	✪✪✪✪
Group	✪
Fun	✪

5.59 | *Motivational marketing*

Preparation None.
Running time 10 minutes.
Resources Ability to produce posters etc.
Frequency Occasional.

All a company's marketing, from direct advertising to subtle PR, is intended to motivate. Given the apparent power of marketing, it seems reasonable that it should be turned on internal motivation. If you need to get across a strong message, perhaps to support a major change, taking a marketing approach is highly beneficial. You will need to involve professionals – the 10-minute running time on this activity is only to consider the option. You won't motivate with an amateurish poster or poorly written messages. Motivational marketing should be used infrequently, and ought to be regarded as a last resort. However much fun it might be, marketing emphasizes the distance there is between you and those being motivated.

Feedback This approach needs careful handling. One person's motivational slogan can be another's joke. Take a couple of specific examples. A large company, aiming to produce a warm glow in its staff, produced a glossy poster with the slogan 'What was the highest mountain before they discovered Everest?' This was supposed to show how easy it is to jump to the wrong conclusion – the 'correct' answer being 'Everest'. The trouble is, all it ever did for me was to suggest that the true correct answer was 'The highest known mountain of the time' – because perception is more important than absolute reality in such circumstances.

Another example was a department with a bad image, which tried to improve motivation using arty posters carrying slogans like 'I'm improving customer service'. This resulted in a series of pirate posters with negative slogans like 'I'm going downhill fast' accompanying the picture of a skier. Poster campaigns reinforce a message, but don't turn things round – in fact in isolation they are a negative force. Also, when money is tight they can be seen as a waste of money.

Outcome Carefully used and professional marketing will help with a major campaign, but posters and slogans alone can't improve motivation.

Variations None.

Individual	✪✪✪
Team	✪✪✪
Group	✪✪✪
Fun	✪✪

5.60 | *The earnest objector*

Preparation None.
Running time Five minutes.
Resources None.
Frequency Occasional.

The earnest objector is not uncommon in a group exercise. He or she generally has an intellectual outlook and picks up on a point of concern that is genuine, but which most attendees are happy to gloss over. For the objector, however, it causes real discomfort.

A couple of practical examples. Attending a course on presentation skills, the attendees are told that it is better to cancel a presentation than give it when the conditions are poor. Later in the course, each attendee has to give a presentation. The objector refuses to do so, as there are no window blinds and the graphics projector is too weak to be seen properly. In another example, a conference involves a role-play. The objector argues correctly that the role-play is unrealistic because under the circumstances described, those involved would take a totally different course of action. She refuses to take part.

It is tempting to brush over the objection to keep to time – but the objector will be quietly fuming about the situation. Equally ineffective is arguing out the matter in front of the group, which can generate a hostile reaction. Instead, have a five-minute comfort break (don't wait for one) and take the objector to one side to discuss the problem. If his or her view is reasonable, make a concession. If this is not practical in the timescale, explain why and undertake to change in the future. If the view isn't reasonable, explain and if possible give the objector the option to sit out that section.

Feedback An earnest objector is entirely different from a habitual troublemaker (see *Confronting troublemakers*, 5.29). The troublemaker sees little good in anything. The objector is positive, but finds the particular point difficult or simply wrong.

Outcome Demotivation is contagious. Although it may seem overkill to stop a session to sort out an individual, it will be worth it. You may also improve your session – and groups benefit from more frequent breaks than they are usually allowed.

Variations None.

Individual	✪
Team	✪
Group	✪✪✪✪
Fun	✪✪

5.61 | *What did I say?*

Preparation None.
Running time One minute.
Resources None.
Frequency Regular.

A surprising amount of demotivation comes from misunderstanding and misinterpretation. You can deliver a stirring message, seeing only the motivational aspects, and those listening can hear something quite different with disastrous consequences. Take the opportunity when you are communicating to check back on what was heard. Make sure that your key motivational messages were heard at all, and that they put across the feeling that you intended them to. Don't assume – check.

This shouldn't feel like a test, or an attempt to make sure that your audience was paying attention. Ask the recipients to give a summary or to pull it together. You can encourage people to do this without being prompted by testing understanding yourself when people communicate to you.

Feedback This is just as necessary with teams as with individuals. Sometimes there will be reluctance to feed back the message actually within the team meeting. You may well find that a particular individual in the team is good at feeding back the message to you as the team heard it. If this is the case, make use of that individual, but bear in mind that their view will be filtered through their own perceptions, and that if you are seen to listen only to that individual it will suggest demotivating favouritism.

Outcome No matter how clear you think your message is, it has the potential for misunderstanding, transforming it into a force for demotivation. Checking what was heard is essential.

Variations Even large groups should be tested for a response, by a combination of random questioning and feedback forms.

Individual	✪✪✪✪
Team	✪✪✪✪
Group	✪✪✪
Fun	✪✪

5.62 | *Train strain*

Preparation Staff have training.
Running time Five minutes.
Resources None.
Frequency Regular.

While training itself is usually motivational (see *Train tracks*, 5.42), there's an archetypal example of the aftermath of training reducing motivation. It's a familiar scenario to most of us. You come back from a course all fired up with enthusiasm, and get dropped back into your working environment (with one or more days of work to catch up with). There's no time to put all those great ideas into use now, so you put the training notes aside to get back to when the rush is over. And they continue gathering dust until you throw them away.

Most of us recognize how valuable training is, but ought to add the rider 'provided it gets put into practice'. If you can help your staff to make use of their training, you will bring the motivational effect of that training into fruition. First, bear practicality in mind when you book a course. Does it have clear, usable outcomes? If you can find a course that gives away real books rather than handouts, go for it. Books are more likely to be read after the event, and sit visibly on the shelf while handouts moulder in a pile. Second, when the participant comes back, have a couple of minutes chatting about what they got out of it, and how it might be integrated into the working environment. Try to give them the time and space to work that integration.

Feedback The feeling you get in these circumstances is worse than simply having wasted a couple of days – after all, chances are the company were paying for this near-holiday. It's not the wasted time, but the frustration of not being able to put all those great new ideas into practice that grates.

Outcome By the end of the course, 90 per cent of the cost has been expended. Don't waste it (and all the associated motivation) by not allowing the participant to bring their learning back into the workplace.

Variations None.

Individual	✪✪✪✪
Team	✪✪
Group	✪
Fun	✪✪

5.63 | *Recognized authority*

Preparation Consider your authority.
Running time 10 minutes.
Resources Staff.
Frequency Occasional.

This technique appears confusingly similar to *Responsibility* (5.20), but is in fact quite separate. The other technique is about increasing an individual's responsibilities – the tasks and work areas they will ensure get completed. Authority is the accepted ability to take decisions and to authorize (or not) action. As such, authority is a special case of responsibility, but it needs to be considered separately.

Although companies are increasingly less authoritarian, to delegate a degree of authority is still one of the most powerful recognitions you can give to a more junior member of staff. It might involve going to a senior decision-making meeting on your behalf. It might involve taking a decision at a technical or business level. In effect, when you delegate authority you are giving others the ability to act on your behalf, as if they were you.

Feedback Because delegation of authority implies a high degree of trust, it will have an equally high associated motivation – provided that the individual wants this responsibility and that you genuinely do trust them. If you delegate authority then constantly look over their shoulder they will soon lose any motivational value. Beware remaking the decisions for them every time.

Outcome The personal benefit of effective delegation of authority is that it stretches elements of a rare resource (you) well beyond the natural limits. From the point of view of those receiving the authority, it shows very strong trust and gives a degree of power, both of which can be highly motivational to the right individuals.

Variations None.

Individual	✪✪✪✪
Team	✪✪
Group	✪
Fun	✪✪

5.64 | *Playing favourites*

Preparation Produce a list of those you motivate.
Running time 10 minutes.
Resources Notepad.
Frequency Once.

Dealing with people is a delicate balance. We're all human and we come equipped with the full range of emotions, likes and dislikes. Of those you work with there will be some you like more than others. It is inevitable. This assessment exercise will allow you to get a feel for how you deal with this emotional side.

Take a list of those you aim to motivate – people who work for you, your peers, your bosses. Don't worry about groups, this is an exercise about individuals. Being honest with yourself, highlight those you particularly like and particularly dislike.

Now try to highlight those individuals who you think an observer would pick out as your favourites. How much do the two sets correlate?

Feedback Almost everyone who deals with people will be seen to have favourites. If you aren't, the chances are you are being too impersonal in your interactions. The secret of using this motivationally is to ensure that your favourites are acknowledged as being such because of what they do, what they deliver, not just because you like them. Often the two will overlap. It's hard not to like someone you work with really well. But on the other hand, it is also possible to really like someone who doesn't deliver. These are the relationships to be particularly wary of.

Outcome You won't be expected to be inhuman, but you are expected to be fair. This includes lack of favouritism, in the sense of favouring someone just because you like them. By getting the right message across you can influence everyone's motivation.

Variations None.

Individual	✪✪✪✪
Team	✪✪✪✪
Group	✪
Fun	✪✪

5.65 | *The hardest cut*

Preparation Staff interviews.
Running time 10 minutes.
Resources Notepad.
Frequency Occasional.

This toughie faces everyone who totally changes the direction of a group. You might be a new manager, or there might be a major switch in strategy. If this isn't your circumstance now, try the exercise anyway, but use a major hypothetical change. The exercise involves thinking through what you would do – the reality takes much longer.

When you have got to know the staff, and the staff understand the changes they are facing, talk to them individually. Make sure they appreciate the need for change, and how it will affect them. As a result of these interviews and picking up general talk in the group, you may find, especially in a long established group, that some individuals simply won't buy in. The caring manager's view is that, with lots of attention, these people will come round. Unfortunately, experience shows this isn't the case. These people will continue to undermine the new direction, demotivating everyone around them. This is an example of where the leader's view is harsher than the manager's. The manager, seeing people as interchangeable components, says 'I can make them work that way'. The leader, recognizing real differences between people, says 'I've given them a chance, but they are sabotaging the change'. And the leader gets rid of them. This sounds brutal. It doesn't have to be. A properly managed career session will help the individual to go in a new direction, and they should be given every support, but they must not be allowed to remain and destroy motivation. Don't let this process drag on either. If they are still there after six months, you have failed.

Feedback I've managed a change of this sort three times. Each time this part of the exercise has been most painful – but has proved necessary. I ought to say also that, apart from this aspect, being an agent of change can be very exciting.

Outcome This is nothing less than essential surgery, yet most of us don't learn this until we've made the mistake of trying to manage without it.

Variations None.

Individual	✪✪✪
Team	✪✪✪✪
Group	✪
Fun	✪

5.66 | *Objective view*

Preparation None.
Running time Five minutes.
Resources None.
Frequency Regular.

Clear, visible objectives can be an excellent motivator. For individuals and teams they provide a guide against which to measure activity. Does it contribute to our objectives? If not, why are we doing it? Having clear, mutually understood objectives can obviate many communications problems and gives a reassuring sense of knowing where we are and where we are going. A frequent mistake with objectives is regarding them as set in concrete. Once you've got your objectives laminated on a plastic card, they're dead. While some will be long-term, some ought to apply to 'this week' and 'this month'. Spend five minutes jotting down your team objectives, if you haven't already listed them, and put them somewhere public.

This technique is just as valuable for large groups. Objectives should be made clear when inviting attendees, so there can be no misunderstanding of the purpose of the event. Someone who is let down by not getting what they expect can be disruptive. This doesn't mean that you can't have plenty of surprises in a session, simply that the underlying objectives should be understood.

Feedback The conditional 'can be' in the first sentence reflects the fact that well-understood objectives won't motivate unless they are felt desirable by those they are shared with. If you are getting together with staff to discuss how to shed half their jobs, don't expect huge motivation at this stage (although it is possible to end up with greater motivation in the remnant). However, there are some intermediate cases where demotivation can be turned round. This is often the case with involuntary developmental training. Some attendees will feel demotivated. They understand the course's objectives, but don't understand the value of those objectives. Some early work showing the practical value – selling the course to them – will reap significant benefits.

Outcome 'Why are we here?' might be a heavy philosophical question, but at the mundane level it's essential for getting a positive approach and contribution.

Variations None.

Individual	✪✪✪✪
Team	✪✪✪✪
Group	✪✪✪
Fun	✪✪

5.67 | *Simple recognition*

Preparation None.
Running time One minute.
Resources None.
Frequency Regular.

In *Public praise* (5.31) we consider the motivational effect of praising someone in front of their peers. Usually this requires an element of planning. However, one-to-one recognition is something that can be given with little or no notice. A simple comment can have a totally disproportionate effect on motivation. It's hard to believe, but extra cash in the pocket doesn't motivate as much as genuine recognition.

When a particularly good job has been done, try to arrange for casual recognition from someone important in the company. Certificates and awards are very nice, but they don't have the same impact as personal contact outside of a formal environment.

Feedback It's important that the person giving the recognition is respected by the recipient. If a technical expert is complimented on technical ability by someone he or she believes has no technical knowledge, the result may well be ineffective. The response is coloured by the thought 'But what does he (or she) know?' Respect multiplies up the value of recognition, so you need to know enough about the person being recognized to have a fair idea of who he or she would respect. If handled well, you can get extra benefit from a 'chance' meeting with a senior person in the company. If, say, a director comes up to the person to be recognized in the corridor and says 'Great job, Phil', there's the added benefit of literal recognition. The individual is extra-motivated by knowing that a director knows him (assuming he is called Phil!). This technique has to be used with care – the senior person needs to be good at appearing to know (or even better, actually knowing) staff before they are let loose.

Outcome Recognition costs nothing but a few potentially embarrassing seconds saying the words (any embarrassment will go with practice) and can result in a major boost of motivation.

Variations Recognition has a weaker but still valuable effect as the numbers involved get larger and larger. The more personal, the better.

Individual	✪✪✪✪
Team	✪✪✪
Group	✪✪
Fun	✪✪✪

5.68 | *Into focus*

Preparation None.
Running time 30 minutes.
Resources Facilitator.
Frequency Occasional.

One way to assess the level of staff morale, and what they feel would increase motivation, is to employ focus groups. These bring together a group of people and a facilitator, who leads them through a discussion of how they are feeling about the company, their job or whatever aspect of motivation you wish to cover.

Focus groups are particularly good at winkling out issues – more so than surveys and questionnaires. The group action allows for ideas to be bounced off other people with different viewpoints, refining them and improving them. Such a process benefits particularly from having cross-functional groups, although technical problems may need a tightly-sourced group. The facilitator should make sure that a wide range of issues is covered. He or she needs to leave the group with a clear contract of what will be done with the information and how the outcomes will be fed back.

Feedback Resist the temptation to save money and do it yourself. The focus group facilitator should be from outside your team – ideally outside the company altogether, or the results you get will be highly-biased towards appearing loyal.

Sometimes a focus group can exaggerate or underplay an issue, where the group's perception is out of balance with that of the company. However, to succeed in motivating those individuals, it will be necessary at least to educate them out of this misapprehension, so this is no disadvantage.

Outcome Effective use of a focus group will identify and lead to the fixing of many issues, and will give those involved the feeling that they are contributing to the way things are done. Make sure everyone has the opportunity to be involved in some group if they want to, though – being excluded is very demotivating.

Variations There are a number of ways focus groups can be organized – as regular small get-togethers, as a major exercise as part of a company-wide session, departmentally, at a team level, and so on.

Individual	✪✪✪✪
Team	✪✪✪✪
Group	✪✪✪
Fun	✪✪

5.69 | *The F word*

Preparation None.
Running time Five minutes.
Resources None.
Frequency Regular.

Motivation and fun go together like… two things that go together very well indeed. In everything we do, fun bubbles through as a reflection of motivation, and the fact of enjoying ourselves feeds back into the motivational loop. It is, therefore, particularly sad that the Victorian values underlying most businesses preclude fun in the workplace. Gradually this is ceasing to be the case. It's certainly very different in startups and some high-tech companies (not all though), where working incredibly hard is balanced with plenty of fun.

Make a regular date to think about how to bring a bit of fun into the working lives of those you motivate. How you do this will depend on the individuals. Some might react very well to a come-to-work-in-silly-clothes day, or a topical limerick competition on the company intranet. Others prefer their fun to be a little more sophisticated (although don't allow them to shut things down for the rest of us). Anything you can do to make work more fun, but that doesn't actually get in the way, will be enhancing.

Feedback Author and consultant David Firth has made a major study of fun in the context of work. See Chapter 6 for more details.

Outcome Fun is something we all deserve and is one of the greatest natural motivators. Why should it be excluded from work?

Variations None – make sure you do it.

Individual	✪✪✪✪
Team	✪✪✪✪
Group	✪✪✪✪
Fun	✪✪✪✪

5.70 | *Banishing bureaucracy*

Preparation None.
Running time 10 minutes.
Resources None.
Frequency Occasional.

Bureaucracy develops within practically any grouping of people. What starts out as a set of sensible procedures to get things done, rapidly and inexorably becomes a frustrating end in its own right. Frustrating is the keyword here – bureaucracy is uniquely demotivating without any balancing benefit.

Occasionally – perhaps quarterly – have a 10-minute anti-bureaucracy session with one of your workgroups (this might be your team or your peers, for instance). Spend a couple of minutes identifying particularly worthless bureaucracy, then pick off a couple of the most irritating examples and develop some solutions.

Someone (not necessarily you) should be tasked with attempting to get the solution in place and reporting back within an agreed timescale.

Feedback Simply recognizing the existence of bureaucracy and attacking it helps, but getting something changed has the most positive benefit. In some circumstances, the apparent bureaucracy will have a sensible and unavoidable reason behind it (for example, a legal safety requirement). If so, the outcome should be to make sure everyone understands just why it is really necessary. Other examples will be capable of simple reform. But don't ignore the class of problem that it isn't possible to change in the short-term (or from your position), but which can simply be avoided by cheating. There's nothing wrong with going round the bureaucracy to get something done, provided it really is bureaucracy.

Outcome This is a great target, as beating a piece of bureaucracy both helps to improve motivation and has a positive effect on the running of the company.

Variations None.

Individual	✪✪✪✪
Team	✪✪✪✪
Group	✪
Fun	✪✪✪

5.71 | **Managing George**

Preparation None.
Running time Five minutes.
Resources None.
Frequency Once.

Are you frustrated by your manager? If not, skip this one. Don't let it drag on. Put together an action plan for changing your relationship through motivation.

- Are there opportunities to get on a better social footing? It might help relationships.

- Can you openly discuss things? Don't assume you can't have a discussion on the meta-level of 'How we do things round here'.

- Find out what motivates your manager. For example, if he or she has a real dislike of paperwork, but you need to get things signed, make it ridiculously easy to do.

Feedback   Why 'Managing George'? I was once managed by 'George'. I enjoyed being managed by George. But everyone else got extremely frustrated. 'How do you cope?' they would say. It was partly because I liked George – you can cope with a lot when you like someone. And the rest was motivation, some of which came from George. He was prepared to give you a task and let you get on with it, making sure you got the reward if it went well. Some came from me. I realized early on that George would only do something if *he* was interested in it. Despite being aware of this, I regularly fell into the trap of forgetting motivation and trying to play it by the book – but the failures from this approach were infrequent enough for me to be quite happy being managed by George.

Outcome   Motivating upwards is never easy (see 5.21 for more general tips), but particularly so with George. Even so, the benefits are even greater.

Variations   Don't forget George's demotivators, too.

Individual	✪✪✪✪
Team	✪✪
Group	✪
Fun	✪✪

5.72 | *The body politic*

Preparation None.
Running time 10 minutes.
Resources None.
Frequency Once.

Office politics are inevitable in large companies, but they can have a devastating effect on motivation. It seems the only way to eliminate office politics is to get rid of large companies (usually, the smaller the company, the less politics involved). While this is desirable, it's outside the scope of this book. What you can do is to assess objectively your own involvement, and to get a feel for political stresses amongst your staff.

Typical signs of office politics in action are sly comments, spreading rumours, the formation of cliques and looking for ways to gain power other than doing the job well. Be honest about yourself. It might seem quite innocent to pass on a rumour about someone else, for example. Yet such political action diverts efforts from work and is divisive. Spend a few minutes jotting down anything you do that is office politics and how you will avoid it. It's only when you are happy that you don't practise politics that you can sensibly discourage others – otherwise you will rightly be seen as hypocritical.

Feedback There isn't an exact definition of office politics, so act carefully. A spectrum runs from politics, through playing the system to getting things done despite bureaucracy. While politics is to be avoided, it is in everyone's interest to make sure that bureaucracy doesn't get in the way (see *Banishing bureaucracy*, 5.70). Similarly, don't confuse cliques with networking. Networking – having a wide range of people in the company with whom you can share information and use as interdependent resources – is extremely valuable. The confusion is easy, because the difference is one of feel. Networking is inclusive, positive and work-oriented (although it can have a social aspect). Cliques are exclusive, destructive and personality-oriented.

Outcome Recognizing the existence of politics is a first step, but you can best succeed by example. If you are seen to avoid office politics it will help your staff to do so.

Variations None.

Individual	✪✪✪✪
Team	✪✪✪
Group	✪
Fun	✪✪

5.73 | *Task force opportunities*

Preparation None.
Running time 10 minutes.
Resources None.
Frequency Regular.

We all grow stale in the same job. Sometimes there is enough variety from career progression – in fact, some would appreciate the opportunity to sit in the same seat for six months at a time – but for many a lack of variety and challenge results in gradual dulling of motivation. A good way to return to sharpness is making use of task forces. Typically these bring together a cross-functional team to tackle a specific task. Task forces might be full time, with secondment from the existing job, or part time.

On a regular basis, and when you are aware of an initiative in the company, consider the staff you are responsible for and the opportunities for task force work. The motivational factors are significant and varied. A new role, working with different people, a more exciting atmosphere than normal office life, a specific challenge (for many administrators, a real demotivating factor is the lack of specific objectives, there's just more of the same) and clear arrival.

Feedback It's often the case when on a part-time task force that the staff member is expected to do everything they did before as well. If you are to have someone involved, they should be able to offload some of their responsibilities in the interim. A full-time secondment always has a degree of uncertainty about there still being a job to come back to. It may well be that they won't return to the same job (in fact, it's a good idea not to, as it may seem very stale), but there should be a clear path for getting one when the task force ends.

Outcome Task force places aren't in everyone's gift, but if you can get some of your staff involved in them, you will find a real boost to their motivation.

Variations Even if you can't get someone into a task force you may be able to find other special, short-term tasks with specific endings for them.

Individual	✪✪✪✪
Team	✪✪
Group	✪✪
Fun	✪✪✪

5.74 | ***No secrets***

Preparation None.
Running time 10 minutes.
Resources None.
Frequency Once.

To put this technique into practice you need to be quite senior in the company, or to be able to get an idea reasonably high up the tree.

Secrets are demotivating; being open and honest is a real positive asset. But you knew that. So why do you keep so many things secret? Consider this course of action. Put all your personnel details, including pay, in open filing cabinets that anyone can access – or publish them on the intranet. Make sure you do it properly. No exceptions. And full disclosure – all your rewards, please, directors.

Feedback The first reaction to this proposal is shock. You *can't* do this. It will result in anarchy and confusion. Yet it's exactly what computer consultancy CMG and engineering firm Semco do. And the result is positive motivation. It takes a little while to get used to, but it eliminates the rumours, suppositions and petty concerns over parity with other staff.

Of course it also implies implementing your reward system extremely fairly, but you are doing that anyway, aren't you? It will temporarily demotivate some people, who find they are doing less well than others they think they're better than. Discuss this with them. Make sure they understand why they aren't so highly rated, and what they can do about it. Turn it into an opportunity for motivation.

Outcome Any non-benefits from personal irritation will be far outweighed by the benefits of trust and openness. This is a bold step, but has great potential to make a difference.

Variations Look at other 'confidential' information and make sure that it really won't endanger the company if it is more widely known. The more information about the company you get to the staff, the more motivated they will be to give their best, and the better chance they'll have of delivering on it. Read Ricardo Semler's *Maverick!* (see Chapter 6) for ways to go even further.

Individual	✪✪✪✪
Team	✪✪✪✪
Group	✪
Fun	✪✪

5.75 | *Golden bull*

Preparation None.
Running time 10 minutes.
Resources None.
Frequency Occasional.

Now and again it is a good idea to review your motivational processes with a golden bull detector. This needn't take long. Look through the means the company has at its disposal to reward good performance and to motivate. Look out for anything that has the feeling of 24-carat, gold-plated-style plastic. You know the sort of thing – it would make you cringe if it was sitting on your mantelpiece. It's not something you'd want to show off to your friends. Yet, all too often, it's exactly what we like to give away to recognize performance. Guard against it.

Feedback This isn't a diatribe against certificates and trophies. Just the need to distinguish between those you'd put on your wall and those you'd hide in your cupboard. The whole point of this form of visible recognition is that it should be displayed, but all too often it looks as if the designers had the taste areas of the brain surgically removed.

It's not an easy decision, because in the area of reward we are closest to children, and have our most child-like tastes. Yet sophistication is often sadly lacking from this area – and it wouldn't do any harm to introduce some.

Outcome Some people really don't care about this one, but some do – and as motivation is about dealing with individuals it's up to you to decide whether you ought to be sourcing your certificates and trophies from a more sophisticated catalogue. It's certainly a mistake to assume that glitz equals supremacy – for instance, the degree certificates of Oxford and Cambridge, universities with more than a little prestige, are less fancy than those of practically any other British university.

Variations This appreciation of the understated is particularly high in the UK, the Scandinavian/Germanic parts of Europe and the Eastern seaboard of the USA. If you are dealing with other parts of the world, you may need to change your views to match local culture.

Individual	✪✪✪✪
Team	✪✪✪
Group	✪✪✪
Fun	✪✪✪

5.76 | *Chunky incentives*

Preparation None.
Running time 10 minutes.
Resources Budget.
Frequency Occasional.

Spend a few minutes thinking about the value of large incentives. While they pall with over-frequent use (as can be seen in some specialist occupations), generally the thought of a big incentive is motivational. In fact, most of the motivation comes from the anticipation, rather than the delivery of the incentive itself.

One clear area where this applies is in lump sum bonuses. I have consulted for a company that seriously felt that bonuses in the region of £100–£200 (perhaps 0.2 to 0.3 per cent of annual salary) would be motivational. Such a bonus verges on the insulting. If that's the amount of money you want to spend, you'd be much better using an appropriate gift (see *Gift aid*, 5.11). A meaningful lump sum should be at least a week's salary and typically closer to a month's. An alternative to lump sums is the use of a major item – a car, a luxury holiday, etc as an incentive.

Feedback You might not have the control over the budget that would allow large incentives. This doesn't mean that you can't lobby for them. One of the best ways of doing this is to move to a company reward scheme in which a reasonably high proportion of the salary is given as a performance bonus. If you don't have such a scheme (for all staff, not just managers), start lobbying for one.

One way you can provide the potential anticipation of a big incentive within the capability of any budget is to use lottery tickets as quick 'thank you' motivators. You may need to check with your company to make sure that the legal people don't have any objection to this.

Outcome You may not be able to give major incentives all the time, or to many people, but bearing in mind it is the anticipation rather than the delivery of the incentive that improves motivation, the occasional big incentive can be valuable, as long as everyone genuinely has a chance of getting them.

Variations None.

Individual	✪✪✪✪
Team	✪
Group	✪
Fun	✪✪✪

5.77 | *Isolate to motivate*

Preparation None.
Running time 10 minutes.
Resources Quiet room(s).
Frequency Once.

Teamworking is great, but even the most gregarious person benefits from having somewhere quiet to go. It might be just to think, it might be to develop a new concept or to fill out some fiddly details. Even if the person you are trying to motivate has their own office, a quiet room will help them to get away from phone calls and drop-in visitors.

This exercise is about establishing a quiet room collection. Most buildings have a number of appropriate rooms. Unless you are very lucky, you won't have one at your sole disposal, but if you do own a meeting room, make sure that it is available to your staff for quiet times. Otherwise, go hunting. Are there meeting rooms for general use that can be booked? Note them down. Are there empty rooms between roles? Find out how to get into them. Are there other rooms that don't get much use? Gain access. There may even be quiet spaces around your site that aren't rooms in the conventional sense – be aware of them. Once your quiet room collection has been built up, give the people you are trying to motivate access to it.

Feedback There can be a concern that quiet rooms are going to be used simply for relaxation. If the lack of trust this implies is justified, make sure that the quiet rooms have glass walls.

In a team environment, other members of the team might find it frustrating that they can't get hold of the individual in the quiet room. Make it easy on a regular basis to get hold of someone if it's urgent – say by having half-hourly break points.

Outcome The ability to get some personal space is an essential for everyone. Providing a quiet room says that you value what the individual does – a highly motivational message – and ensures that tasks are more likely to get completed, again motivational.

Variations Consider allowing home working and other flexible working patterns as an alternative to the quiet room.

Individual	✪✪✪✪
Team	✪
Group	✪
Fun	✪✪

5.78 | *What's in it for me?*

Preparation None.
Running time Five minutes.
Resources None.
Frequency Regular.

Underlying an understanding of motivation is the ability to put yourself into someone else's shoes and ask 'What's in it for me?' Of course, this isn't the sole driver of the human spirit – in fact, time and again under pressure other factors win out over personal gain – but taking this viewpoint can be a valuable check on your motivational input, especially when dealing with a large group. If you are planning a group session, think yourself into the mind of Isobel, a typical attendee. Perform a crude cost–benefit analysis. What would she have been doing if she wasn't attending? What is it costing her to attend? What will she get out of it personally or in status? What would she enjoy anyway and what is she merely attending out of loyalty?

Surprisingly, often when undertaking such exercises, the benefits come at a remarkably high price. If you want to maximize motivation, look for opportunities to reduce costs and improve personal benefits for Isobel. You can also increase benefits for the company or the country or the world, but they will generally have significantly less impact on motivation.

Feedback The cost aspect isn't entirely straightforward. Bear in mind the opportunity cost – the cost of missing what could have been done. This can be particularly strong if attendees are self-employed, where attending a day's session means a day without earnings.

Outcome You're never going to get entirely into someone else's mindset, and you will often be dealing with a group of very different people, so the concept of a 'typical' person may be difficult to pin down. This does not make the exercise less valuable, though.

Variations This approach is essential with group sessions. It is less so with individuals and teams where you will normally have more information and a longer relationship – but it is always valuable to see a force like motivation from the viewpoint of the recipient.

Individual	✪✪✪
Team	✪✪✪
Group	✪✪✪✪
Fun	✪✪

5.79 | *Ambience chasers*

Preparation None.
Running time Five minutes.
Resources None.
Frequency Once.

Spend a few minutes on an ambience review. Look at the environment of the person or people you are trying to motivate. Is it pleasant? Is it comfortable? Is it personal? When you consider ambience from the viewpoint of a participant, you often come across distressing truths. For example, let's say you were managing a supermarket, trying to motivate shoppers. Consider the checkout. There's nowhere to sit, there's nothing to read but the covers of glossy magazines, nothing to entertain you and not so much as a pot plant. You might make similar observations about a person sitting on a hard seat in an auditorium, or the hapless Dilbert in Scott Adams' masterful cartoons, stuck in his demotivating cubicle.

Ambience problems aren't necessarily easy to fix. You can't put seating at a supermarket checkout because there isn't room and it would get in the way of the trolleys. There have to be hard seats in that particular auditorium because they can't afford to replace them. Dilbert has to have his cubicle to fit with company policies. Yet these are all excuses, and the creative manager can overcome them.

Feedback If beauty is in the eye of the beholder, ambience is in the senses of the experiencer (it just doesn't sound as good). While there are some reasonably universal requirements – a comfortable temperature, for example, that doesn't freeze you or put you to sleep – many aspects of ambience are personal. What may be intolerable mess to one person could be cosy surroundings to another. When working at a group level you have to work at a generic level, though.

Outcome Ambience can have a startlingly strong effect on motivation. Generally it does so when other motivational factors are weak – if you are really interested in what you are doing, you won't care where you do it. Even so, ambience should be ignored at your peril, especially if you are in a competitive area like supermarket checkouts.

Variations None.

Individual	✪✪✪
Team	✪✪✪
Group	✪✪✪✪
Fun	✪✪

6

MORE MOTIVATION

FINDING OUT MORE

Motivation is a broad subject. While *Instant Motivation* gives you an excellent programme for improving your motivation skills and the motivation of those around you, it is an area that is worth delving into further. The references below provide information on books for improving motivation.

An easy way to get hold of many of the recommended books is through the Creativity Unleashed online bookshop, which specializes in business and creativity books – see **www.cul.co.uk/books**

BOOKS

GENERAL

John Allan (1996) *How to be better at motivating people,* Kogan Page
An Industrial Society-backed guide to motivation. Good use of case studies and tips make this an excellent choice if you want to expand on the background in the opening chapters of *Instant Motivation*.

Richard Denny (1993) *Motivate to Win*, Kogan Page
Don't be put off by the relative age of this book, the content hasn't dated. Denny has a very charismatic approach to motivation, and puts the message across well. It's a personal approach, so some may not like it – but it's worth a look.

David Firth (1995) *How to make work fun*, Gower
David Firth's book explores the whole area of fun and work much more fully than is possible here. The A–Z format seems a little forced occasionally, but makes it easy to dip into. While not always directly practical, it's a great source of inspiration.

Patrick Forsyth (1998) *30 Minutes to Motivate Your Staff*, Kogan Page
Part of a pocketbook series putting across the basics of the subject – handy if you'd like a bit more than our introductory chapters can give, but haven't time for a Denny or an Allan.

Robert Heller (1998) *Motivating People*, Dorling Kindersley
A handy pocket guide to motivation in the heavily illustrated DK style. Some of the approaches are a trifle old-fashioned, but overall a good pocket introduction to the subject.

Michael Leapman (1987) *The Last Days of the Beeb*, Coronet
Leapman's inside view of the BBC before the major reorganizations that turned it into a modern business is a classic case study in how not to motivate. Well worth reading.

Ricardo Semler (1994) *Maverick!*, Arrow
One of the best books ever written about motivation. It's not a textbook, but the biography of a company. Despite being located in Brazil during runaway inflation and with potentially difficult unions, Semler took a disgruntled workforce and totally changed their motivation by making their workplace a place where they wanted to be.

TEAM

Paul Birch (1999) *Instant Leadership*, Kogan Page
A companion volume in the Instant series, *Instant Leadership* provides a wide range of techniques to improve leadership skills. An essential for improving team motivation, these exercises combine instant focus with longer-term development.

Brian Clegg and Paul Birch (1998) *Instant Teamwork*, Kogan Page
The first book in the Instant series, *Instant Teamwork* contains a wealth of exercises to help to get a team working better together. The quick-to-use ice-breakers, warm-ups and timeouts are designed to break down barriers between individuals and put energy into a team's efforts. By making a team work together more effectively they make an excellent contribution to the team's motivation.

TIME MANAGEMENT

Brian Clegg (1998) *The Chameleon Manager*, Butterworth Heinemann
This book takes the concept of time management into the wider sphere of gaining the skills needed to thrive in the workplace of the new millennium. It identifies management of creativity, communication and knowledge as the key requirements to working your way, and includes a different slant on time management from this perspective.

Brian Clegg (1999) *Instant Time Management*, Kogan Page
A companion volume in the Instant series, *Instant Time Management* provides a host of techniques for improving your time management without taking too much time over it. Good time management enables you to deliver on your promises and ensure that your motivational programme is carried through – with poor time management, however good your intentions, you can fail to motivate.

Marion E Hayes (1996) *Make Every Minute Count*, Kogan Page
In the quick-fire 'Better Management Skills' series, this is the only one of these books that is US-written – but the subject varies little between countries. Even more checklists and questionnaires than Smith's book, this is an excellent way of getting started in the subject.

Ted Johns (1994) *Perfect Time Management*, Arrow
A handy pocketbook giving an overview of time management practice from a very pragmatic viewpoint. Varies between background and quite a lot of detail (eg suggested forms for the agenda of a meeting.

Lothar J Seiwert (1989) *Managing Your Time*, Kogan Page
A very visual book with lots of diagrams and plans and cartoons – it'll either impress you (as it has apparently more than 300,000 readers) or leave you cold. Particularly helpful if you like very specific guidance and information as juicy snippets.

Jane Smith (1997) *How to be a Better Time Manager*, Kogan Page
An Industrial Society-sponsored volume, Smith's book takes an easy-to-read, no-nonsense approach to time management. A fair number of check lists and little questionnaires to fill in along the way, if you like that style.

APPENDIX: THE SELECTOR

THE RANDOM SELECTOR

Take a watch with a second hand and note the number the second hand is pointing at now. Take that number technique from the list of 60 below.

No.	Ref.	Title	No.	Ref.	Title
1	5.1	It's catching	31	5.43	Peerless peers
2	5.2	Somewhere to go	32	5.46	No comment
3	5.3	Demolishing demotivators	33	5.48	Empty desk syndrome
4	5.4	Publish and be damned	34	5.49	Change as motivator
5	5.5	Arrivals	35	5.50	The genuine article
6	5.6	Risk and failure	36	5.51	The rumour mill
7	5.7	Contributors	37	5.52	Absolute sports
8	5.8	Eye eye	38	5.53	Quality content
9	5.9	Tooling up	39	5.54	Faking it
10	5.10	Stretch but don't stress	40	5.55	Spice it up
11	5.11	Gift aid	41	5.56	Team supporters
12	5.12	Do it themselves	42	5.57	Toys for boys
13	5.14	Understanding your style	43	5.58	Two-faced management
14	5.15	Meeting motivation	44	5.59	Motivational marketing
15	5.16	Perspective shift	45	5.61	What did I say?
16	5.17	Energy transfer	46	5.62	Train strain
17	5.18	A little note	47	5.63	Recognized authority
18	5.20	Responsibility	48	5.64	Playing favourites
19	5.21	Looking up	49	5.65	The hardest cut
20	5.22	Money, money, money	50	5.66	Objective view
21	5.23	Daggers drawn	51	5.67	Simple recognition
22	5.25	Time counts	52	5.68	Into focus
23	5.26	Portfolio matching	53	5.69	The F word
24	5.27	The tea bag	54	5.70	Banishing bureaucracy
25	5.30	Promises, promises	55	5.72	The body politic
26	5.34	Visible improvement	56	5.74	No secrets
27	5.35	Smashing the suggestion box	57	5.76	Chunky incentives
28	5.36	E-motivation	58	5.77	Isolate to motivate
29	5.37	Ask them	59	5.78	What's in it for me?
30	5.41	Celebration time	60	5.79	Ambience chasers

TECHNIQUES IN TIMING ORDER

This table sorts the techniques by the suggested timings. Those at the top take the longest, those towards the bottom are the quickest.

Ref.	Title	Ref.	Title
Evening		*Five Minutes*	
5.41	Celebration time	5.5	Arrivals
30 Minutes		5.7	Contributors
5.16	Perspective shift	5.8	Eye eye
5.19	Appropriate appraisal	5.10	Stretch but don't stress
5.49	Change as motivator	5.14	Understanding your style
5.68	Into focus	5.15	Meeting motivation
15 Minutes		5.18	A little note
5.3	Demolishing demotivators	5.20	Responsibility
5.13	Share and enjoy	5.21	Looking up
5.32	Change control	5.28	Critical response
5.56	Team supporters	5.33	Travel broadens the mind
10 Minutes		5.34	Visible improvement
5.1	It's catching	5.36	E-motivation
5.2	Somewhere to go	5.38	Lasers and dry ice
5.4	Publish and be damned	5.39	Break time
5.6	Risk and failure	5.40	Firm but fair
5.9	Tooling up	5.43	Peerless peers
5.11	Gift aid	5.44	Warm-ups
5.12	Do it themselves	5.45	Personal projects
5.22	Money, money, money	5.46	No comment
5.23	Daggers drawn	5.47	Own pocket
5.24	Fill in the form	5.48	Empty desk syndrome
5.26	Portfolio matching	5.54	Faking it
5.29	Confronting troublemakers	5.55	Spice it up
5.35	Smashing the suggestion box	5.57	Toys for boys
5.37	Ask them	5.58	Two-faced management
5.42	Train tracks	5.60	The earnest objector
5.50	The genuine article	5.62	Train strain
5.51	The rumour mill	5.66	Objective view
5.52	Absolute sports	5.69	The F word
5.53	Quality content	5.71	Managing George
5.59	Motivational marketing	5.78	What's in it for me?
5.63	Recognized authority	5.79	Ambience chasers
5.64	Playing favourites	*Two Minutes*	
5.65	The hardest cut	5.17	Energy transfer
5.70	Banishing bureaucracy	*One Minute*	
5.72	The body politic	5.25	Time counts
5.73	Task force opportunities	5.27	The tea bag
5.74	No secrets	5.30	Promises, promises
5.75	Golden bull	5.31	Public praise
5.76	Chunky incentives	5.61	What did I say?
5.77	Isolate to motivate	5.67	Simple recognition

TECHNIQUES IN FREQUENCY ORDER

This table sorts the techniques by the frequency order. Those at the top are undertaken most frequently, those at the bottom once only.

Ref.	Title
Regular	
5.4	Publish and be damned
5.5	Arrivals
5.6	Risk and failure
5.7	Contributors
5.10	Stretch but don't stress
5.17	Energy transfer
5.18	A little note
5.25	Time counts
5.27	The tea bag
5.28	Critical response
5.30	Promises, promises
5.31	Public praise
5.33	Travel broadens the mind
5.36	E-motivation
5.39	Break time
5.53	Quality content
5.55	Spice it up
5.61	What did I say?
5.62	Train strain
5.66	Objective view
5.67	Simple recognition
5.69	The F word
5.73	Task force opportunities
5.78	What's in it for me?
Occasional	
5.2	Somewhere to go
5.3	Demolishing demotivators
5.9	Tooling up
5.11	Gift aid
5.15	Meeting motivation
5.16	Perspective shift
5.19	Appropriate appraisal
5.20	Responsibility
5.21	Looking up
5.24	Fill in the form
5.26	Portfolio matching
5.29	Confronting troublemakers
5.32	Change control
5.38	Lasers and dry ice
5.40	Firm but fair
5.41	Celebration time

Ref.	Title
5.42	Train tracks
5.43	Peerless peers
5.44	Warm-ups
5.45	Personal projects
5.47	Own pocket
5.49	Change as motivator
5.57	Toys for boys
5.59	Motivational marketing
5.60	The earnest objector
5.63	Recognized authority
5.65	The hardest cut
5.68	Into focus
5.70	Banishing bureaucracy
5.75	Golden bull
5.76	Chunky incentives
Twice	
5.50	The genuine article
Once	
5.1	It's catching
5.8	Eye eye
5.12	Do it themselves
5.13	Share and enjoy
5.14	Understanding your style
5.22	Money, money, money
5.23	Daggers drawn
5.34	Visible improvement
5.35	Smashing the suggestion box
5.37	Ask them
5.46	No comment
5.48	Empty desk syndrome
5.51	The rumour mill
5.52	Absolute sports
5.54	Faking it
5.56	Team supporters
5.58	Two-faced management
5.64	Playing favourites
5.71	Managing George
5.72	The body politic
5.74	No secrets
5.77	Isolate to motivate
5.79	Ambience chasers

TECHNIQUES IN APPLICABILITY TO INDIVIDUAL ORDER

This table sorts the techniques by the individual star ratings attached to each. Those at the top have the highest star rating, those at the bottom the lowest.

Ref.	Title
✪✪✪✪	
5.2	Somewhere to go
5.3	Demolishing demotivators
5.4	Publish and be damned
5.5	Arrivals
5.6	Risk and failure
5.7	Contributors
5.8	Eye eye
5.9	Tooling up
5.10	Stretch but don't stress
5.11	Gift aid
5.12	Do it themselves
5.13	Share and enjoy
5.14	Understanding your style
5.15	Meeting motivation
5.16	Perspective shift
5.18	A little note
5.19	Appropriate appraisal
5.20	Responsibility
5.21	Looking up
5.22	Money, money, money
5.23	Daggers drawn
5.24	Fill in the form
5.25	Time counts
5.26	Portfolio matching
5.27	The tea bag
5.28	Critical response
5.29	Confronting troublemakers
5.30	Promises, promises
5.31	Public praise
5.32	Change control
5.33	Travel broadens the mind
5.34	Visible improvement
5.35	Smashing the suggestion box
5.36	E-motivation
5.37	Ask them
5.42	Train tracks
5.43	Peerless peers
5.45	Personal projects
5.46	No comment
5.47	Own pocket

Ref.	Title
5.48	Empty desk syndrome
5.49	Change as motivator
5.50	The genuine article
5.51	The rumour mill
5.54	Faking it
5.56	Team supporters
5.58	Two-faced management
5.61	What did I say?
5.62	Train strain
5.63	Recognized authority
5.64	Playing favourites
5.66	Objective view
5.67	Simple recognition
5.68	Into focus
5.69	The F word
5.70	Banishing bureaucracy
5.71	Managing George
5.72	The body politic
5.73	Task force opportunities
5.74	No secrets
5.75	Golden bull
5.76	Chunky incentives
5.77	Isolate to motivate
✪✪✪	
5.39	Break time
5.40	Firm but fair
5.41	Celebration time
5.55	Spice it up
5.57	Toys for boys
5.59	Motivational marketing
5.65	The hardest cut
5.78	What's in it for me?
5.79	Ambience chasers
✪✪	
5.17	Energy transfer
5.38	Lasers and dry ice
5.52	Absolute sports
✪	
5.44	Warm-ups
5.53	Quality content
5.60	The earnest objector

TECHNIQUES IN APPLICABILITY TO TEAMS ORDER

This table sorts the techniques by the team star ratings attached to each. Those at the top have the highest star rating, those at the bottom the lowest.

Ref.	Title
✪✪✪✪	
5.1	It's catching
5.4	Publish and be damned
5.5	Arrivals
5.6	Risk and failure
5.7	Contributors
5.9	Tooling up
5.10	Stretch but don't stress
5.14	Understanding your style
5.22	Money, money, money
5.23	Daggers drawn
5.24	Fill in the form
5.25	Time counts
5.29	Confronting troublemakers
5.30	Promises, promises
5.34	Visible improvement
5.40	Firm but fair
5.41	Celebration time
5.44	Warm-ups
5.49	Change as motivator
5.50	The genuine article
5.51	The rumour mill
5.52	Absolute sports
5.58	Two-faced management
5.61	What did I say?
5.64	Playing favourites
5.65	The hardest cut
5.66	Objective view
5.68	Into focus
5.69	The F word
5.70	Banishing bureaucracy
5.74	No secrets
✪✪✪	
5.8	Eye eye
5.12	Do it themselves
5.15	Meeting motivation
5.16	Perspective shift
5.18	A little note
5.20	Responsibility
5.27	The tea bag
5.31	Public praise
5.36	E-motivation

Ref.	Title
5.37	Ask them
5.39	Break time
5.42	Train tracks
5.43	Peerless peers
5.47	Own pocket
5.48	Empty desk syndrome
5.55	Spice it up
5.56	Team supporters
5.57	Toys for boys
5.59	Motivational marketing
5.67	Simple recognition
5.72	The body politic
5.75	Golden bull
5.78	What's in it for me?
5.79	Ambience chasers
✪✪	
5.3	Demolishing demotivators
5.11	Gift aid
5.17	Energy transfer
5.19	Appropriate appraisal
5.28	Critical response
5.32	Change control
5.35	Smashing the suggestion box
5.38	Lasers and dry ice
5.45	Personal projects
5.46	No comment
5.54	Faking it
5.62	Train strain
5.63	Recognized authority
5.71	Managing George
5.73	Task force opportunities
✪	
5.2	Somewhere to go
5.13	Share and enjoy
5.21	Looking up
5.26	Portfolio matching
5.33	Travel broadens the mind
5.53	Quality content
5.60	The earnest objector
5.76	Chunky incentives
5.77	Isolate to motivate

TECHNIQUES IN APPLICABILITY TO GROUPS ORDER

This table sorts the techniques by the group star ratings attached to each. Those at the top have the highest star rating, those at the bottom the lowest.

Ref.	Title
✪✪✪✪	
5.1	It's catching
5.10	Stretch but don't stress
5.17	Energy transfer
5.24	Fill in the form
5.25	Time counts
5.30	Promises, promises
5.38	Lasers and dry ice
5.39	Break time
5.41	Celebration time
5.44	Warm-ups
5.50	The genuine article
5.53	Quality content
5.55	Spice it up
5.57	Toys for boys
5.60	The earnest objector
5.66	Objective view
5.69	The F word
5.78	What's in it for me?
5.79	Ambience chasers
✪✪✪	
5.4	Publish and be damned
5.7	Contributors
5.8	Eye eye
5.29	Confronting troublemakers
5.56	Team supporters
5.59	Motivational marketing
5.61	What did I say?
5.68	Into focus
5.75	Golden bull
✪✪	
5.5	Arrivals
5.9	Tooling up
5.28	Critical response
5.31	Public praise
5.36	E-motivation
5.47	Own pocket
5.67	Simple recognition
✪	
5.2	Somewhere to go
5.3	Demolishing demotivators
5.6	Risk and failure

Ref.	Title
5.11	Gift aid
5.12	Do it themselves
5.13	Share and enjoy
5.14	Understanding your style
5.15	Meeting motivation
5.16	Perspective shift
5.18	A little note
5.19	Appropriate appraisal
5.20	Responsibility
5.21	Looking up
5.22	Money, money, money
5.23	Daggers drawn
5.26	Portfolio matching
5.27	The tea bag
5.32	Change control
5.33	Travel broadens the mind
5.34	Visible improvement
5.35	Smashing the suggestion box
5.37	Ask them
5.40	Firm but fair
5.42	Train tracks
5.43	Peerless peers
5.45	Personal projects
5.46	No comment
5.48	Empty desk syndrome
5.49	Change as motivator
5.51	The rumour mill
5.52	Absolute sports
5.54	Faking it
5.58	Two-faced management
5.62	Train strain
5.63	Recognized authority
5.64	Playing favourites
5.65	The hardest cut
5.70	Banishing bureaucracy
5.71	Managing George
5.72	The body politic
5.73	Task force opportunities
5.74	No secrets
5.76	Chunky incentives
5.77	Isolate to motivate

TECHNIQUES IN FUN ORDER

This table sorts the techniques by the fun star ratings attached to each. Those at the top have the highest star rating, those at the bottom the lowest.

Ref.	Title	Ref.	Title
✪✪✪✪		5.16	Perspective shift
5.1	It's catching	5.19	Appropriate appraisal
5.17	Energy transfer	5.20	Responsibility
5.26	Portfolio matching	5.21	Looking up
5.27	The tea bag	5.22	Money, money, money
5.33	Travel broadens the mind	5.24	Fill in the form
5.38	Lasers and dry ice	5.25	Time counts
5.41	Celebration time	5.28	Critical response
5.44	Warm-ups	5.30	Promises, promises
5.57	Toys for boys	5.32	Change control
5.69	The F word	5.36	E-motivation
✪✪✪		5.37	Ask them
5.4	Publish and be damned	5.43	Peerless peers
5.5	Arrivals	5.46	No comment
5.9	Tooling up	5.48	Empty desk syndrome
5.10	Stretch but don't stress	5.49	Change as motivator
5.11	Gift aid	5.50	The genuine article
5.13	Share and enjoy	5.51	The rumour mill
5.18	A little note	5.53	Quality content
5.31	Public praise	5.56	Team supporters
5.34	Visible improvement	5.59	Motivational marketing
5.35	Smashing the suggestion box	5.60	The earnest objector
5.39	Break time	5.61	What did I say?
5.42	Train tracks	5.62	Train strain
5.45	Personal projects	5.63	Recognized authority
5.47	Own pocket	5.64	Playing favourites
5.52	Absolute sports	5.66	Objective view
5.55	Spice it up	5.68	Into focus
5.67	Simple recognition	5.71	Managing George
5.70	Banishing bureaucracy	5.72	The body politic
5.73	Task force opportunities	5.74	No secrets
5.75	Golden bull	5.77	Isolate to motivate
5.76	Chunky incentives	5.78	What's in it for me?
✪✪		5.79	Ambience chasers
5.2	Somewhere to go	✪	
5.3	Demolishing demotivators	5.23	Daggers drawn
5.6	Risk and failure	5.29	Confronting troublemakers
5.7	Contributors	5.40	Firm but fair
5.8	Eye eye	5.54	Faking it
5.12	Do it themselves	5.58	Two-faced management
5.14	Understanding your style	5.65	The hardest cut
5.15	Meeting motivation		

The Instant Series

Titles available are:

Instant Brainpower, Brian Clegg
Instant Creativity, Brian Clegg and Paul Birch
Instant Leadership, Paul Birch
Instant Motivation, Brian Clegg
Instant Stress Management, Brian Clegg
Instant Teamwork, Brian Clegg and Paul Birch
Instant Time Management, Brian Clegg

Available from all good booksellers. For further information on the series, please contact:

Kogan Page
120 Pentonville Road
London
N1 9JN
Tel: 020 7278 0433
Fax: 020 7837 6348
e-mail: kpinfo@kogan-page.co.uk

or visit our Web site: www.kogan-page.co.uk

Visit Kogan Page on-line

Comprehensive information on
Kogan Page titles

Features include

■ complete catalogue listings,
  including book reviews and
  descriptions

■ on-line discounts on a variety
  of titles

■ special monthly promotions

■ information and discounts on
  NEW titles and BESTSELLING titles

■ a secure shopping basket facility
  for on-line ordering

■ infoZones, with links and
  information on specific areas of
  interest

PLUS everything you need to know
about KOGAN PAGE

http://www.kogan-page.co.uk